Christopher Sorrentino
Death Wish

CHRISTOPHER SORRENTINO is the author of three novels, including *Trance*, a finalist for the National Book Award. His work has appeared in *Bomb*, *Bookforum*, *Esquire*, *Granta*, *Harper's Magazine*, *McSweeney's*, *The New York Times*, *Playboy*, and many other publications. He lives in Brooklyn.

Deep Focus

also available in this series:

They Live by Jonathan Lethem

Deep Focus

Death Wish

Christopher Sorrentino

Series Editor, Sean Howe

Soft Skull Press | New York

Library of Congress Cataloging-in-Publication Data
Sorrentino, Christopher, 1963–
    Death wish / Christopher Sorrentino, edited by Sean Howe.
        p. cm.
Includes bibliographical references and index.
ISBN 978-1-59376-289-6 (alk. paper)
1. Death wish (Motion picture : 1974) I. Howe, Sean. II. Title.
PN1997.D3775 S67 2011
791.43'72—dc22

                                    2010029076

Cover design by Spacesick
Interior design by Elyse Strongin, Neuwirth & Associates, Inc.
Printed in the United States of America

Soft Skull Press
New York, NY

www.softskull.com

For Sean Howe, Andrew Hultkrans, and Jonathan Lethem

[H]e commits himself to the forest primeval; there, so long as life shall be his, to act upon a calm, cloistered scheme of strategical, implacable, and lonesome vengeance. Ever on the noiseless trail; cool, collected, patient; less seen than felt; snuffing, smelling—a Leather-stocking Nemesis. In the settlements he will not be seen again; in eyes of old companions tears may start at some chance thing that speaks of him; but they never look for him, nor call; they know he will not come. Suns and seasons fleet; the tiger-lily blows and falls; babes are born and leap in their mothers' arms; but, the Indian-hater is good as gone to his long home, and "Terror" is his epitaph.

—HERMAN MELVILLE, *The Confidence-Man*

[A]ny accountant in any American city secretly feeds the hope that one day, from the slough of his actual personality, there can spring forth a superman who is capable of redeeming years of mediocre existence.

—UMBERTO ECO, "The Myth of Superman"

[The Western film] offers a serious orientation to the problem of violence such as can be found almost nowhere else in our culture. One of the well-known peculiarities of modern civilized opinion is its refusal to acknowledge the value of violence. This refusal is a virtue, but like many virtues it involves a certain willful blindness and it encourages hypocrisy. We train ourselves to be shocked or bored by cultural images of violence, and our very concept of heroism tends to be a passive one: we are less drawn to the brave young men who kill large numbers of our enemies than to the heroic prisoners who endure torture without capitulating. In art, though we may still be able to understand and participate in the values of the Iliad, a modern writer like Ernest Hemingway we find somewhat embarrassing . . . And in the criticism of popular culture, where the educated observer is usually under the illusion that he has nothing at stake, the presence of images of violence is often assumed to be in itself a sufficient ground for condemnation.

—ROBERT WARSHOW, "Movie Chronicle: The Westerner"

[T]he sort of project that seems to have been developed without even the intention of being any good.

—SEAN FRENCH, on *The Terminator*

CONTENTS

Death Wish

PROLOGUE

Allowing Our Wits to Take Flight

Vincent Canby had to go back for seconds. The senior film critic of *The New York Times* had reviewed *Death Wish* on July 25, 1974, declaring it to be "a bird-brained movie to cheer the hearts of the far-right wing," and "despicable." Now, in the pages of the Sunday, August 4, 1974, edition of the *Times,* Canby expanded upon his thoughts about the film. Headlined 'DEATH WISH' EXPLOITS FEAR IRRESPONSIBLY, his piece said, in part:

> From the early reports, *Death Wish* is on its way to becoming one of the big dumb hits of the summer season, which is depressing news but not terribly hard to understand. Its powers to arouse—through demonstrations of action—are not unlike those of a pornographic movie.
>
> It cuts through all sorts of inhibitions, first by making us witnesses to the murder and rape of Paul's wife and daughter, graphically and agonizingly shown, thus to certify Paul's (and our) right for vengeance . . . If you allow your wits to take flight, it's difficult not to respond with the kind of lunatic cheers that rocked the Loews Astor Plaza when I was there the other evening. At one point a man behind me shouted with delight: "That'll teach the mothers!"

Although what really is "difficult" is to dispel the impression of a self-styled highbrow slumming amidst the masses, Canby's complaint is informed only slightly by his bruised æsthetic sensibilities (the quoted passage actually makes an unwitting argument for the film's effectiveness *qua* film); mostly he is motivated by moral outrage, a highly selective outrage that isolates the film from its antecedents (the only other movies Canby mentions are Alan Arkin's film version of the Jules Feiffer play *Little Murders* and one of director Michael Winner's three earlier films with Charles Bronson, *The Mechanic*), thereby isolating it from film itself, the better to condemn it on extra-cinematic grounds (an act, really, of critical misfeasance).

Stern charges of moral impropriety (and political turpitude) have always been leveled at individual films—just a few years earlier the Don Siegel/Clint Eastwood film *Dirty Harry* had been denounced as "fascist medievalism" by Pauline Kael, a critic of far more enduring persuasiveness than Vincent Canby (fascism was invoked also by Roger Ebert and others to characterize Siegel's anti-determinist fable). *Death Wish* became a sitting duck for critics who saw in the film a political agenda that precisely matched what they found most objectionable.[1] But even if *Death Wish* is easily picked off for

---

1. As Robert B. Ray suggests in his book *A Certain Tendency of the Hollywood Cinema, 1930–1980*, such criticisms often are themselves skewed politically, with the "liberal" individualism of films that veer to the left (he mentions *Bonnie and Clyde*, *Butch Cassidy and the Sundance Kid*, and *The Wild Bunch*) more likely to be accepted at face value, and applauded, than that of similarly violent (and often more coherent) films belonging to what he calls the "Right Cycle" (e.g., *Death Wish*, *Dirty Harry*, *Walking Tall*).

its politics—or, rather, what we imagine its politics to be—it continues to exist as film, as the sum of its performances, in the coherence of its script, its place in a larger context, the provocations it offers its viewers. But, other than the provocations—which many reviewers wrote about as if they were immune to them—critics avoided discussing these subjects. Canby announced—glibly, for Canby's pronouncements on *Death Wish* are undercut by his insufferable superiority to the material he was treating—that New York "has its problems: bad bookkeeping, polluted air, rising costs, reduced services, high crime rates, a fleeing middle class. Now you might want to add a movie to the list, Michael Winner's *Death Wish*." Really? If New York's "problems" are different today, is *Death Wish* itself still a problem? Does a film's value mutate along with the reality to which we seek to compare it? Is that what we mean by a "period piece"? *Death Wish* is a frozen pose, a piece of popular art, one that reveals a bygone zeitgeist without in any true way reflecting the society that sustained it. Of course New York wasn't the way *Death Wish* depicts it. (Nor, for that matter, were Tucson and Hawaii, the movie's two other locales: as John Shelton Lawrence and Robert Jewett note in *The Myth of the American Superhero*, crime statistics in both places were roughly comparable to those of New York at the time.) Muggers didn't operate that way, the police didn't operate that way, psychosis doesn't occur that way, and the theme of revenge is simply too interesting for a film to turn it into a second job the way this one does.

But criticism begins to unravel as soon as it insists that the reflection a movie casts is distorted. "Realism" is never exactly that, and in the case of *Death Wish*, realism wasn't even the intention. We forget that film is where negative capability found its most welcoming home, "without any irritable reaching after fact & reason." What Canby refers to disapprovingly as allowing "your wits to take flight" is the fundamental filmgoing experience. (And it's interesting to read the mandarin certitude of those critics who report on the audiences' reactions at screenings; their refusal to honor that unanimity, the communion of those dark rooms, is telling, even impeaching. You want to tell them simply that they're looking in the wrong direction.) Rather than acknowledge (or recognize) that, critics challenged us at the level of the schoolyard taunt: if you like this, you're stupid.

It's a likable film, though, and I'm not stupid. It's also a film that perfectly realizes its own invented form, but then becomes incoherent; a nasty provocation, but one that somehow doesn't go quite far enough; a superb exploitation of an actor's limitations, but a film full of stilted performances; an interestingly photographed depiction of a nightmare city, but a film whose director sometimes seems to lose interest in what's happening on the screen; an influential film, but one that begot an almost entirely tedious genre (the worst examples of which possibly are its own sequels). This rickety instability can in itself keep you interested: Is *Death Wish* a good movie that ultimately fails, or is it a bad movie that succeeds brilliantly from time to time? Could it be both?

I've structured this book as a series of discrete chapters (they can be read as individual essays, almost) that break *Death Wish* down into some of its constituent elements. There is overlap and, because I sometimes look at the same thing more than once but in different contexts, there are contradictions, all of which occur in an effort to explore the movie's various ways of being, and to dig it out from under the prejudices that have buried it since its release.[2]

---

2. For those unfamiliar with the film or who wish to refresh their memory of the details of its plot, a full synopsis is included as an appendix.

1

Death Wish and the City

The New York of *Death Wish* announces itself via a negative proposition: it is most decidedly not Hawaii, the paradise where Paul and Joanna Kersey have lately been vacationing— a place so paradisical, in fact, that even during tourist season the beach on which we first glimpse them is deserted, enough so that Paul suggests that he and Joanna have sex there. "We're too civilized," Joanna responds, the more ironic of two express references to civilization made in the film. Here the film hooks us into a simple binary argument that it will make repeatedly: urbanism, civilization, is a destroyer of joy, of potential, of life; the pastoral—in the film's formulation, resort hotels and, later on, exurban developments—allows one to "live." To be ideally "uncivilized," in addition to permitting you to fuck on the beach, is to be freed of your inhibitions against righteous murder. This isn't merely an inference on my part: the second reference to civilization in the film, when Paul articulates his ideas about self-defense to his son-in-law, makes this point explicitly. By then Joanna is in the ground and Paul's daughter is in the nuthouse: See what all that civilization got them?

Joanna's voicing a lament: she does not want to go home—to civilization—and who, after all, would want to leave this Hawaii? Hawaii's elision is as carefully planned as anything in the film. It is sun, surf, sand, swaying palms. It is Eden as conceived by a God who wears white patent leather shoes and a floral shirt. Such a Hallmark romance is it, that nearly the only natural thing in the landscape is Charles Bronson himself, his astonishing physique.

We're often treated to the somewhat ill-considered conceit that "the city itself" is the protagonist of a given work of art. It's a facile idea, and usually not one that makes much sense to me. (We never hear, for example, that the stage set, the landscape, is the protagonist of a Beckett play, although those environments of his often seem to have at least as much agency as his hapless characters.) But the city-as-protagonist conceit serves as shorthand indicating the presence of a kind of authenticity, and it follows that such a protagonist-city would be well-rounded, believable, *real*.

But the city in film is always a dream. That dream may cohere around humdrum production requirements, the act of making virtue of necessity (the nonsensical, to anyone who has lived there, route the car chase takes through the streets of San Francisco in *Bullitt*), or around arch, self-reflexive contrivances (Scorsese's *New York, New York*), but the film that always fails is the one that denies the dream, that struggles to impose the very logic and order of the street grid on its portrayal. There's a sort of schematic, unimaginative reasoning to that: Put a camera on the sidewalk and *voila*! The city! That documentary refusal of synthesis can become very tiresome, especially if you grew up in New York and know what a Sabrett cart looks like, what a tenement hallway looks like, what a streetwalker looks like, how a *cafone* talks, what black girls arguing sounds like, what piles of dirty snow and slush amassed near intersections look like—I could go on and on. Gathering such intelligence is novice's work. Falling in love with that intelligence is a novice's mistake. But that mistake is irresistible sometimes. William Friedkin made it. Sidney Lumet never learned not to. Four decades into his career, Scorsese still seems torn between lush fabrication and the facile vocabulary of "authenticity." One of the great refreshing strengths of *Death Wish* is Michael Winner's lack of interest in taking a documentary approach to New York City. It's as if, armed with data identifying the place as the center of urban anomie (which, granted, it was in the popular imagination), he arrived, established his few locations, and began shooting (so to speak). Most of it could have been filmed on the back lot (indeed, Charles Bronson, reluctant to leave his home in Southern California for weeks of shooting in New York, reportedly lobbied to have the location changed to Los Angeles), and the carnivalesque scenes in the film—complainants at a police precinct, prostitutes at a coffee shop—seem rote, tired. *Death Wish*'s peculiar dream exists at the expense of local color: New York is a cave into which predators can crawl. Bronson discovers himself in the cave.

Death Wish never announced itself as a realistic film. Consider the irony in the voice-over accompanying the trailer:

> Enjoy a typical afternoon in New York City. This is Paul Kersey. This is the story of a man who decided to clean up the most violent town in the world. He begins where all the

supercops leave off. Call him a mad vigilante. Call him a hero. Either way, he's always on target. Never make a death wish. Because a death wish always comes true. And you get to love it.

This copy seems to have been lifted wholesale from the utterances of some comedian specializing in verbal free fall—the performances of Jonathan Winters come to mind—and in light of its sheer wackiness I'm left to wonder, for a moment, what reviewers might have made of *Death Wish* if Winner and his screenwriter, Wendell Mayes (whose career had included work on several films by Otto Preminger, as well as those of Billy Wilder, Henry Hathaway, and Delmer Daves), had explicitly foregrounded the fantasy elements of the film; conceiving of Paul Kersey as a kind of modern Dr. Van Helsing, or setting the movie in a New York of the not-so-distant future—say, 1984 (still, at that point, a loaded date).[3] I raise this speculation only because Canby praised, somewhat lavishly, both *A Clockwork Orange* and *Escape from New York*, two films whose pure objectionableness, at least by the standards he brought to *Death Wish*, can have been ameliorated only by the fact of their having been set in the "future." Or reversed—what if *Death Wish* had been set in the Hollywood West whose myths it expressly quotes?

---

3. Strangely, although the film makes no effort to present a New York that is "futuristic" in any way, the inference wasn't difficult to draw. Roger Ebert wrote, "[T]his doesn't look like 1974, but like one of those bloody future cities in science-fiction novels about anarchy in the twenty-first century." Canby himself said, with oddly arbitrary specificity, "The New York City shown in *Death Wish* looks to be about three years from now."

(Canby's response to Clint Eastwood's *High Plains Drifter* was indulgently charitable: "part ghost story, part revenge Western, more than a little silly, and often quite entertaining," he wrote, although then he added, "in a way that may make you wonder if you have lost your good sense." Canby apparently *never* wanted to allow his wits to take flight.)

As it was, the most vehement objections to *Death Wish* were grounded in an idea that the movie sought or purported to present "realism," and that in doing so it either fell far short, or outright lied. That's a very general encapsulation of the varied responses to the film, but no discussion of *Death Wish*'s ostensible politics, attitudes, and exhortations (which were the predominant focus of contemporary commentators) could proceed from the idea that *Death Wish* is a *fantasy*, from an acknowledgment of it as fiction. The premise that the film was a dangerous lie depended upon its establishment as an attempted representation of reality.

I was born and raised in New York City, and when talking about this project, some people have asked me: Was New York in 1974 "like" *Death Wish*? The quickest answer is no. But then, I could say the same about the New York seen in any number of Woody Allen films. Allen's frame of reference is at least as cramped as Winner's, and the anxious link he forces between the complex splendor of Manhattan and his utterly arrested, Great Books 101 conception of erudite sophistication seems to me more sophomoric than anything in *Death Wish* (I will note here without further comment that Allen's great and early champion was . . . Vincent Canby). But I digress. One reason the film is patently uninterested in depicting a New

York full of spicy smells and sweaty tumult (or, *pace* Allen, the Thalia theater and Elaine's) is because it is bent not on recreating an actual city but on evoking the familiar nightmare of being trapped in a strange and threatening place. People who actually lived in New York didn't go around cringing in fear all the time; if anything, *Death Wish* projects the external fears of non-city-dwellers on its urban characters. At that point in time, New York was the focus of national (e.g., FORD TO CITY: DROP DEAD) anti-urban hostility. For non–New Yorkers, the film was almost certainly the embodiment of a leviathan they never, or only fleetingly, had seen (the old joke holds true; New York is a great place to live, but you wouldn't want to visit there). To just rattle off the names of notorious urban dead zones—Newark, Cleveland, Detroit, Baltimore—or even those forsaken parts of New York that most middle-class New Yorkers never thought about (the South Bronx, East New York) is to appreciate how ludicrously *unreal* it was to set the locus of the urban id on Riverside Drive.

New Yorkers knew that we were watching someone else's dream. We also knew, vaguely perhaps, that we were being insulted. But movies are vastly democratic that way: to watch someone else's dream is to assume its logic, its imponderables; to be caught in its flow along with the dreamer. We knew that it was not New York we were seeing, but "New York."

Besides, by the 1970s such insults had become commonplace. An honest avenger (or reformer) arrives in town to clear something up. We see it in *Klute*. We see it in *Serpico*. We see it in *Coogan's Bluff*. We see it turned on its head in *Taxi Driver*. Or a contagion arrives from without and a local hero must step outside the commonplace to contain it, wending his way through a gallery of colorful but stereotypical "types." We see that in *The French Connection*, and in *The Taking of Pelham One Two Three*, and in *No Way to Treat a Lady*. Or the "types" themselves are the focus of the film, whether amid an intensely focused crisis (*Dog Day Afternoon*) or an episodic voyage (*Midnight Cowboy*).

New York very good-naturedly stood for fear, alienation, crime, violence, illicit sex, garrulous ethnicity. It always had. All those things are present in *Rear Window*, way back in 1954. But Hitchcock filmed that on a specially constructed set, on a soundstage in California. It was flattering and different to see the city's streets in film after film—not just those above, but dozens of others of the era, films as different as *Bye Bye Braverman* (Lumet, 1968), *Little Murders* (Arkin, 1971), *Shaft* (Parks, 1971), *The Hot Rock* (Yates, 1972), *Cops and Robbers* (Avakian, 1973), *Mean Streets* (Scorsese, 1973), *The Seven-Ups* (D'Antoni, 1973), *Harry and Tonto* (Mazursky, 1974), *Law and Disorder* (Passer, 1974), *The Super Cops* (Parks, 1974), *Three Days of the Condor* (Pollack, 1975), *Marathon Man* (Schlesinger, 1976), *Next Stop, Greenwich Village* (Mazursky, 1976)—films whose photography, sound, production design, and performances can sometimes seem slightly generic today.[4]

---

4. Such "gritty" films seem to have been left far behind with the coming of the strange fantasia of New York as a lover's (and consumer's) paradise of gigantic lofts, classic six-room apartments, long walks through Central Park, cabs on every corner—Woody Allen for dummies, or at least without the continual references to items on the syllabus of an Adult Ed liberal studies class.

Suffice it to say that the New York of *Death Wish* was greeted by New Yorkers with a kind of recognition that stood apart from their familiarity with the city in which they lived. We have been watching "New York" on film for a century; its fakeness is affected not at all by whether such film is shot on its streets.

We finally see the city when the silhouettes of its buildings appear against a luridly colored sky (not too different, really, from the colors of the Hawaiian sunset), the movie's title superimposed in the foreground, while Herbie Hancock hits a heavy, buzzing synthesizer chord. "Finally" because Hawaii seems to have taken forever (although the sequence is less than two minutes long). The opening is a fairly elaborate pretense that the film draws us into: *Death Wish* pretends that it would prefer to stay in paradise, and we pretend to agree, but really none of us can wait to get back to hell.

Perfunctory exterior shots of the city track the couple's journey home from the airport in a taxi. Winner's casual attitude toward location shooting sometimes undercuts his own vision: the elevated 7 train rumbling above Queens, the romantic shot of the Fifty-ninth Street Bridge (*two* shots of the bridge, inexplicably, taken from slightly different positions at different times of day, one in particular a romantic "gateway" shot with the sun setting behind Manhattan—a come-on, not a warning), the great intersection at Seventy-second and Broadway; all are enough to establish New York as a working metropolis full of life and energy (which it was). I suspect that Winner shot boilerplate footage to make it absolutely clear to his audience where they were—what it was all *about* would come later on. (The cinematographer, Arthur J. Ornitz, worked on three of the New York-based films—*Serpico*, *Law and Disorder*, and *Next Stop, Greenwich Village*—I list earlier.[5])

Would *Death Wish* be appreciably better, or have been better received, if Winner had selected equally genuine but more obscure and picturesquely run-down locations? It wouldn't have taken much to divert that taxi ride, go through Harlem. That might have denoted a level of craftsmanship (and that all-important authenticity) that could have satisfied reviewers—or, at any rate, that might have fired up the movie-watching synapses that shut down in so many of them when their knees began to jerk toward their chins. To his credit, Canby struggles to express his sense of the film's disdain for authenticity, though he can't come up with it. The best he can manage is to blast it as "a movie produced by tourists," but that's not quite right. Winner doesn't have nearly enough of the tourist's tendency to energetically revel in his knowledge of "secrets," that impulse toward over-embroidery (again, Friedkin comes to mind). Winner's approach to New York is generic: pretty much you see either a postcard view or a set of alleys, paths, staircases, and side streets that could have been found on a back lot.

Besides, what could "Harlem" have had to do with *Death Wish*? There's no room for Harlem or the South Bronx or the Lower East Side or Bedford-Stuyvesant or Brownsville in *Death Wish*. The key to accepting *Death Wish*'s fantasy is

---

5. Ornitz shot only the New York scenes. The uncredited Richard Kline filmed the Hawaii and Tucson sequences.

to accept that crime and violence are scourges visited upon a respectable and peace-loving citizenry from without—a beautiful and convenient myth (and, as we shall see, I use that word advisedly)[6]: if that's the case, then nothing in the world is more complicated than Paul Kersey and his gun. Winner doesn't want New York itself to signify its own subtle meanings and menaces (let alone suggest the socioeconomic roots of those things). A more "realistic" backdrop to the opening credits might include a montage of second-unit shots: ne'er-do-wells loitering menacingly on a street corner, drunks sprawled on the sidewalk, burnt-out and abandoned buildings in any of a dozen neighborhoods—but that might raise questions that would linger irritatingly in the viewer's mind. Winner wants to use the city for one thing only, as the sinister backdrop of a series of mythical confrontations. I remember when I was a kid doing a social studies project on the Aztecs: I dutifully reported on their agriculture and social structure, but really I was in a hurry to get to the heart sacrifices. As far as I was concerned, without heart sacrifices, the Aztecs were nothing. Winner's series of establishing shots here is the equivalent of the agriculture, etc. Exterior location shooting is in fact extremely limited in the

---

6. I am not discounting the fact that many happily continue to confuse reality with a version of this myth. Writing on http: bighollywood.breitbart.com in 2009, S. T. Karnick said, "*Death Wish* marked the death of liberal illusions about crime and punishment: the idea that crime is caused by disadvantageous social environments and that the solution is to pour even more taxpayer money into bad neighborhoods in an attempt to buy submission from the poorer elements of society."

film, when compared with the fetishization of street scenes in some other films of the era: the bulk of the exteriors are shot on the block where the Kersey home at 33 Riverside Drive is located (the entrance is on Seventy-fifth Street) and in a stretch of Riverside Park.

The opening credits conclude quite nicely with a wordless sequence in which we see the everyday habits of life settle once again upon Paul and Joanna: he checks the mail in the lobby of their apartment building, they enter their apartment, Joanna serves a pickup supper while Paul goes through the mail, and finally the couple, their transition from the natural to the civilized complete, goes chastely to bed: blackout. The true nature of this city begins to become clear the next day, when Paul returns to work. His coworker Sam asks him, "Do you know what was happening while you and Joanna were living it up in Maui or Kaui or Yowey or whatever it is? There were fifteen murders the first week, and twenty-one last week in this goddamn city."[7] A moment later, Paul's boss, Ives, asks: "How does it feel to be back in the war zone?" So far, nearly all the dialogue has had the effect of pushing us to agree with the film's assertions about life in "the city." I don't want to go home, there've been thirty-six murders in the two weeks since we've been gone, decent people are going to have to live somewhere else, it's a war zone.

---

7. This reminds me a little of a joke that an old British vaudeville comedian, Robb Wilton, used to tell: "The day war broke out, me missus said to me, 'What're you gonna do about it?'"

This rhetoric is somewhat at odds with the dreamy, oblivious behavior exhibited by ordinary people in public spaces: when, soon after, Joanna goes with her and Paul's daughter, Carol, to the D'Agostino supermarket where they are first spotted and thereafter stalked by the three "freaks" (as they are identified in the credits), led by Jeff Goldblum (his first film role), they and the other shoppers move somnambulistically amid the bright abundant aisles even as the freaks rush manically through the store, yelling and knocking merchandise from the shelves. Again, Winner seems more concerned with overall affect than with contriving an "authentic" scene: the three freaks run, jump, and cavort like three Beatles in a lost scene from *A Hard Day's Night*. But the composure of Joanna and Carol seems less like patient forbearance or conditioned inurement than a comatose lack of awareness. After the two women are attacked in the Kersey apartment, Paul is summoned to the hospital, another interior space whose occupants appear intent on going about their "official" functions despite the chaos (of a different sort) in their midst. There is a remarkable brief shot of a man in the center of the frame, covered with blood, standing in a state of confusion as white-garbed nurses, doctors, and orderlies move around him through the brightly lit white space like water around a rock, then a cut to Kersey watching through a glass partition. "There's a man over there who's bleeding," he says. "And nobody comes." Scenes like this fill the movie: public and semi-public urban spaces in which the denizens of New York are manifestly indifferent to or unaware of the danger and pain surrounding them, paying no attention to the actions that are our sole focus. This is film exploiting and emphasizing our special status as watchers: rather than implicating us in this vast indifference (as Hitchcock might have implicated us), it allies us with Paul, who either is at the center of our attention or is himself intently watching the action. We see it at the hospital, in the police station, at the airport, in the subway. But it's not only we and Paul who are paying attention: in this city, evil also is watching; the innocent blindly go through the motions of normalcy at their peril. Shortly after the attack that's left Joanna dead and Carol catatonic, Paul is sent to Tucson to work on a real estate project that seems poised—due to its developer's impractical ideas, anathema to the sensibilities of coldly calculating Easterners, about real estate development—to lose more money than Paul's company, a potential backer, is willing to risk. This crucial interlude has far more significance than simply affording Paul the opportunity to obtain an unlicensed handgun (as it does in Brian Garfield's source novel): it introduces us to a counter-city, a city where, as Ives says when dispatching Paul there, "people can breathe." Paul meets Ames Jainchill, the builder who evangelizes on behalf of Tucson, development that conforms to the land (even at the expense of maximum profitability), and gun ownership as the cornerstones of a superior way of life. He tells Paul, "A gun is just a tool. Like a hammer, or an axe. Wasn't long ago, used to put food on the table. Keep foxes out of the chicken coop. And rustlers off the range. Bandits out of the bank." This is a remarkable piece of dialogue, taking as it does the mythic differences between sodbusters, ranchers, and the lawless Western town that long served as the raw material for violent conflict in Western movies (one of the posters on the wall of the gun club to which Ames brings

Paul is from *Lawman*—a Michael Winner film that concerns itself with these same differences), and conflating them into a kind of historical unanimity emanating solely from unfettered gun ownership. He goes on: "This is gun country. Can't even own a handgun in New York City. Out here I hardly know a man that doesn't own one. And I'll tell you something: unlike your city, we can walk our streets and through our parks at night and feel safe."

Earlier, Ames has brought Paul to Old Tucson. Although the script archly has him make reference to the fact that "they shoot movies here sometimes," it is in fact a gigantic set—originally constructed in 1939 for the shooting of *Arizona*—and theme park. Here Paul watches, along with a crowd of spectators, a reenactment of an archetypal gunfight between a marshal and three bad guys. Unlike in "New York," the citizenry in "Tucson" pays close attention to the acts of evildoers, and as the marshal shoots the bandits one by one, the citizenry duly applauds each time. To underscore the point, the on-site narrator of the scene intones: *The outlaw life seemed a shortcut to easy money, which could buy liquor, women, and a turn at the gambling table. But there were honest men, with dreams, who would fight to protect their*—here Ames, bored, talks over the spiel to tell Paul, "Let's get that beer"—*and who would plant the roots that would grow into a nation.*

The purpose of the Tucson interlude is ostensibly to show Paul's transformation from frustrated victim into implacable avenger, his shedding of his effete Eastern conditioning to embrace the take-charge solution of individual armed response to the problem of aggression. But more than that, it provides us with an urban arcadia, the perfect balance between the convenience of contemporary urban society and the purported values (and the allowable expediencies) of an earlier time. "Muggers operating out here, they just plain get their asses blown off," says Ames. It also, via scenes depicting Paul hard at work solving the pro-blem of making the Jainchill development profitable while retaining Ames's ideal of remaining true to the land and providing "space for life" (including a wordless sequence, scored by Hancock like one of those scenes from a Western in which some arduous but redeeming task is undertaken, where we see Paul on the site, staking out lots, surveying land, taking notes, and consulting with engineers and contractors over blueprints), shows him internalizing the values that contrast so sharply with those of back home (while effectively transferring our own identification from the old values to the new). Despite Paul's explaining to Jainchill that he served as a conscientious objector in Korea, that his pacifist and nonviolent tendencies were cemented when his father died in a hunting accident—the first time a family member met a violent end—by the time Ames hands him a pistol at the gun club, the die has been cast.

After successfully completing the Jainchill assignment, Paul returns to New York, unaware that stowed in his suitcase is a .32-caliber revolver. Ever the evangelist, Jainchill has tucked the gift-wrapped pistol in Paul's luggage as a "going-away present": Paul will now spread the blow-their-asses-off gospel of Gun Country to New York. After having been confronted with the upsetting news that Carol's condition has grown worse during his absence and that fancy-pants New York doctors continue to be helpless to improve it—could a missing piece in *Death Wish* be a Tucson hospital scene or, better, an old-fashioned house call, in which a simple country doctor performs a medical miracle (perhaps to heal Paul of his blindness)—and with the arrival in the mail of the photographs he and Joanna had taken on their vacation, Paul discovers the gun in his bag and immediately recognizes his missionary assignment. As Daniel Boone said of himself, he has become "separated from the cheerful society of men . . . an instrument ordained to settle the wilderness" of New York. (Truly, he has become Charles Bronson.) He goes to nearby Riverside Park, where, true to the nightmare logic of the film, he is confronted by an armed mugger within moments, and commences the killing spree that dominates the second half of the movie.

In that second half, the city provides us with a variation on the (not then) old argument that we "weren't allowed" to win in Vietnam (an analogy that, now that I think of it, intimates the wealth of subtexts that must have been resonantly present when the film was released). Ames Jainchill has made clear that individual safety in the West is guaranteed by a right to self-protection unhampered by government, and the performance in Old Tucson has shown that lawful authority ideally gives no quarter when coping with crime; now Eastern authority reveals a correspondingly weak and dissembling nature. The district attorney and the police commissioner, personifying the city administration, express fear that citizens will follow Paul's lead by taking the law into their own hands, and suppress the information that crime has dropped since his actions have become known. The scene (which takes place in the district attorney's luxuriously appointed office, as the two well-dressed officials munch on candy from a crystal dish) in which they inform the rumpled and hardworking Inspector Frank Ochoa, who is on the verge of cracking the case, that while he must stop Paul he is not to arrest him makes clear that the only real concern of city officials is in maintaining the consolidation of their own power. (Like the parallels with a frustrated war effort, the depiction of high officials conspiring to lie to us must have had special resonance in that summer when a president fell victim to his own resolute and chronic dishonesty.) It's a pretty subtle take on the backroom politics that might govern such a situation: a movie possessing the blunderbuss sensibilities that *Death Wish* has often been accused of might have granted Ochoa an audience with the mayor himself (cf. *Dirty Harry*), but in fact no politicians are seen in the movie (a headline is briefly seen that reads "STOP VIGILANTE" MAYOR DEMANDS), unless you count the district attorney (although New Yorkers are well aware that this tends to be a position of lifetime tenure). The implication is that these men, who answer not to the citizenry but to a higher organizational authority (and their own ambition), are facing pressure from above.

And also from the media: there is another, arch component of the city in *Death Wish*: throughout the second half of the film, once news of the vigilante has broken, press and television reports constantly punctuate the film. The administration is very conscious of being Creon to Paul's Antigone; the district attorney says, when asked about apprehending Paul, "I don't want a martyr on my hands!" This isn't a facile reference; like Sopho-cles's tragedy, the film is in many ways an exploration of the con-flict between one's obligations to the state and its laws and the need to answer to a higher, or more "natural," law, a need that is ratified and commented on by the media. The city's secret re-sponse to Paul's acts is formulated in awareness of the unofficial response of its citizens, and the media is a chorus of their voices, mostly telegraphed (and amplified) by television reports, news-paper headlines, magazine covers, and billboards; from Alma Lee Brown, an elderly woman who goes after her attackers with a hatpin ("Everybody better look out for me from now on . . . I've been robbed too many times, and I've had enough!"), to Andrew McCabe, a construction worker whose crew "roughed [a mugger] up a little bit before the police came." This city of vox populi is repeatedly seen in remote communion with Paul: they draw strength and resolve from his actions, while he com-pulsively leafs through magazines and newspapers and watches TV news, gaining confidence from their response, which affirms the righteousness of his actions.

Maybe equally important, it affirms our fascination with them. *Death Wish* may "exploit fear irresponsibly," as Canby had it, but what hindsight makes very clear is that it mostly exploits its audience's sanctioned voyeurism and appetite for the lurid that television had enabled at least since Lee Harvey Oswald had been shot by Jack Ruby on live TV, a moment at which any cen-sorial hopes, good-intentioned or not, of braking the medium were forever dashed. Television revealed its essence then as the perpetual promise of the shocking deviation from the script—it could pretend, and still does, to be about scripted entertainment, even scripted "reality," but our expectations remain keyed to the invasion of the normal by the unforeseen (what better, and purer, television has there ever been than the tape of those jetliners plowing into the lower Manhattan skyline?).

And the unforeseen had become regularly scheduled programming. The beaming of moving, audible images from places like Watts, Detroit, and Newark into American living rooms had transformed our idea of the American city—it wasn't Vietnam that had arrived at home so much as a way of seeing that had been midwifed by its depiction on the tube. Assassinations, riots, wars. A few days before Canby's think piece, Congress adopted three articles of impeachment against President Richard Nixon (who would resign four days after the piece ran). All on television. Perhaps even more pertinent, consider that earlier that summer Christine Chubbuck, a Florida newscaster, shot herself in the head during a live broadcast, announcing just prior to the act, "In keeping with Channel 40's policy of bringing you the latest in blood and guts, and in living color, you are going to see another first—attempted suicide." Chubbuck had pulled off a great feat of self reflexive theater. As Wes "Scoop" Nisker famously said, "If you don't like the news, go out and make some of your own." These events were more than merely televised, they *were* television itself, as were the urban woes that *Death Wish* presented in stylized form.

Hollywood's opting for exploitative entertainment was, at least in part, a way of imitating the sheer propinquity television forced between its audiences and the events it depicted, marking one of the industry's final movements, in the years before special effects flattened all affect by making the real fake and the fake real, toward a deeper naturalism, a naturalism that for the first time took for granted that our most common experiences are mediated experiences. *Death Wish* is a movie profoundly aware of the relationship between events and the way in which they become news, and, covered as news, are distorted and influenced by their own newsworthiness to become stories. Bronson indeed goes out and "makes some of his own."

I wrote earlier of the city in *Death Wish* as a "cave into which predators can crawl." I'd like to elaborate a little, at the risk of contradicting myself slightly. The New York of *Death Wish* is in fact two cities: the first, which exists aboveground, is where conversation, dining, announcements, arrivals, business, gatherings, and so forth take place, usually in well-lit and unthreatening, if not especially welcoming, spaces. Portals to the "other" New York—to the cave—are well marked and found everywhere: subway entrances, the boundaries of city parks, the mouths of alleys. Significantly, the limits are known to all, and generally are observed by both surface- and cave-dwellers.[8] The movie's plot is set in motion by an act

---

8. Not entirely a fabrication. In September 1976, Muhammad Ali and Ken Norton fought for the heavyweight championship at Yankee Stadium. Outside the ballpark, gangs of teenagers robbed and harassed the mostly white and affluent ticket holders, vaulting barricades and trying to crash the stadium gates. Facing disciplinary action for his failure to contain the rampage, Chief Anthony V. Bouza, commanding officer in the Bronx at the time, caused an enormous stir when he was quoted as saying, "The kids impinged on the consciousness of more prominent Americans. If I failed, it's because I didn't continue to make these feral children invisible to middle- and upper-class Americans who aren't used to seeing them."

of trespass: Joanna and Carol haven't gone strolling through Central Park at midnight, ridden the long express stretch between 59th and 125th Streets on the A train, or taken a shortcut through a dark alley. They've observed the tacit rules; it's the "freaks" who've violated them. It's a very superficial reading of the film to assert, as several reviewers did, that the New York of *Death Wish* is overrun by violent criminals, a premise that actually characterizes several of the more prestigious (or, at any rate, less scrutinized) films I've mentioned.

In postulating a violated transaction—the freaks were supposed to have been waiting for their victims to wander into the cave—*Death Wish* carries forward the themes and motifs of the Western films to which it's made explicit reference, films that often depend on a similar violation of established codes of behavior to set their tales of revenge in motion: an insistence not on law, exactly, but order. Garfield's novel has Paul railing to himself and others about his thwarted "right" to walk anywhere he pleases in the city, a realistic and sensible complaint in the real world, but in a movie that conceives of its setting as a "war zone" no such right can be assumed to exist. Charles Bronson is obliged to track the cave-dwellers down where they live to restore order. Both he and the criminals are acting outside of the law, but as the champion of order, Bronson discovers himself, fighting his war of containment. (Vietnam does shimmer, ghostlike, at the edges of this film . . . as does the future War on Terror, in which the original "evildoers" will be all but forgotten.) The contemporary city—even a mythical one—is the only conceivable setting for a story like this. It is not a mere *transliteration* of the fabled West, but a *translation* arising from devolution: if we say that the peak of the Western's arc was its metafictional awareness of the inevitable arrival of the rule of law (as in *The Man Who Shot Liberty Valance*), then in *Death Wish* the gradual ebbing of the law's effectiveness is projected forward into real time, and backward to its urban Eastern origin, to a common point at which, once again, order is the best that can be hoped for.

2

Death Wish and Politics

What are the politics of *Death Wish*? Paul Kersey is described as a liberal. This is made clear in exactly two exchanges, the first near the beginning of the film, when Paul mildly rebuts his colleague Sam's assertion that "decent people" are going to have to live outside of New York City by responding, "By 'decent people' you mean people who can afford to live somewhere else," and Sam replies, "You are such a bleeding-heart liberal, Paul"; and then when Ames Jainchill, having learned that Paul was a conscientious objector during the Korean War, opines that he's "probably one of them knee-jerk liberals who thinks us gun boys shoot our guns because it's an extension of our penises."

Of what does Paul Kersey's knee-jerk, bleeding-heart liberalism consist? Why, of knee-jerk liberal thoughts and bleeding-heart feelings. The movies have a long history of offering tautology as a complete philosophical gesture, of course. Genre would be on shaky ground without it; so much in film depends on our grasping a context in which things simply are what they are, and one is grateful, frequently, for Hollywood's adumbration of certain tedious but necessary elements of narrative.[9] Paul's politics are explained, but reductively, so that the explanation touches on only the origin of his antipathy toward guns: despite an almost preternatural facility with them arising from his having grown up with guns, "all kinds of guns," Paul has forsworn the use of them after his father's death in a hunting accident. "Some fool mistook him for a deer, you see," he tells Ames. From this, all manner of liberal ideas can be presumed to have taken root, exemplified by his service as a conscientious objector, and his admission that he has a heart that "bleeds a little for the underprivileged."

It's impossible for all but the looniest of observers not to agree to bleed a little themselves, since Paul's ideological foil is his colleague Sam, prone to advocating such things as taking those underprivileged and "stick[ing] them in concentration camps"—a toxic suggestion even more loaded, if anything, back in 1974. This is likely a hedge on the movie's part—Paul's eventual vigilantism seems moderate compared to the espousal of such government extremism—but not an especially necessary one, since neither Paul's liberalism nor Sam's conservatism is all that intriguing. In the formulation

---

9. Do we ever, for example, learn more about the Empire in the *Star Wars* films (the original trio, anyway) than that it is evil? The Empire's politics, and most of its habits, remain obscured. Tom Carson, in his essay "Jedi Uber Alles," writes that "it's not too hard to imagine that well-known cinema addict Hitler watching *Star Wars* with tears dripping down his cheeks until they soaked his mustache. He'd simply equate the Jedi with the Aryans, and the Empire with Jewish capitalists and the powers that imposed the Treaty of Versailles on Germany after World War I . . . nothing in the film's schema would prevent him from doing so." Indeed.

of the film, it doesn't matter if a liberal fires the gun and the conservative only talks the talk: a movie like *Death Wish* needs to reserve its important distinctions not between modes of thought but between modes of response.

(That we can't imagine Sam with a gun in his hand, putting food on the table and keeping rustlers off the range, is not irrelevant. As played by William Redfield, Sam, kvetching like an armchair Obersturmbannführer, isn't a candidate for a mythical journey. A lot of reviewers [as well as Garfield, author of the source novel] bitched about the casting of Charles Bronson in the role of Kersey, which seems to me to disingenuously miss the point. Just as it was obvious that Jimmy Stewart would be the one to bring the rule of law to Shinbone in *The Man Who Shot Liberty Valance*, it also was obvious that John Wayne would be the one to lay the violent groundwork.)

The assumption many critics seem to start with is that Paul's vigilantism is antithetical to his liberalism, that his transformation into a vigilante cleanses him of liberalism, and that, ergo, the film is irresponsibly endorsing a certain extreme form of conservatism. I'm not so sure about that. "Liberal" is merely a convenient signifier indicating the starting point of Paul's journey; there's no corresponding end point that spells "conservative" (as much as conservatives may have delighted in the picture). Just as there's very little here to indicate the content of Paul's initially liberal character, there's little to suggest that Paul will from now on enter the voting booth and pull the lever for Republican candidates. But would it matter? *Death Wish* is a stew that renders the differences between genres, let alone the differences between contemporaneous political positions, indistinguishable. To object to it on a political basis strikes me as fundamentally puritanical, in the sense that the objection seems to arise from the film's seeming to take—and bestow—too much pleasure in orchestrating its object lessons, such as they are. But more than anything, the movie's interrogating us, not indoctrinating us.

A comparison with *Dirty Harry*, a film with which *Death Wish* is frequently lumped, is useful. Inspector Harry Callahan's politics are express, even dogmatic. In that movie's emblematic exchange, the district attorney scolds Harry for denying the crazed (and hippie-like) serial killer Scorpio his civil rights: "Where the hell does it say you've got a right to kick down doors, torture suspects, deny medical attention and legal counsel? . . . Does Escobedo ring a bell? Miranda? I mean, you must have heard of the Fourth Amendment . . . that man had rights!" Harry responds, "The law is crazy." We are then introduced to Judge Bannerman, an appellate justice who "holds classes in constitutional law" at UC Berkeley—in 1971, this reference surely must have elicited the desired Pavlovian response—who agrees with the DA, saying, "In my opinion, the search of the suspect's quarters was illegal. Evidence obtained thereby, such as that hunting rifle for instance, is inadmissible in court. You should have gotten a search warrant . . . All evidence concerning the girl, the suspect's confession, all physical evidence, would have to be excluded . . . The suspect's rights were violated under the Fourth and Fifth and probably the Sixth and Fourteenth

Amendments." Callahan responds, "And Anne Marie Deacon, what about her rights? I mean, she's raped and left in a hole to die. Who speaks for her?" *Dirty Harry* does—as would Ronald Reagan, who took up the issue of crime victims' rights early in his first administration. Harry Callahan didn't anticipate the age of Reagan, of course; he was in it: Reagan was at the time governor of California, and it's not difficult to imagine him standing and cheering at a screening of the film. It spoke for him, too, in so many ways.

Death Wish anticipates Reagan only in its lack of detail: the Great Communicator trafficked in feelings and unstated implications far more than he did in policy specifics. It's significant, I think, that Paul Kersey gives no speeches announcing a political change of heart. His only lines treating his arrival at vigilantism are phrased as questions and propositions:

> PAUL: What about the old American social custom of self defense? If the police don't defend us, maybe we ought to do it ourselves.
>
> JACK: We're not pioneers any more, Dad.
>
> PAUL: What are we, Jack?
>
> JACK: What do you mean?
>
> PAUL: I mean, if we're not pioneers, what have we become? What do you call people who, when they're faced with a condition of fear, do nothing about it—they just run and hide?
>
> JACK: Civilized?
>
> PAUL: No.

Granted, this isn't the *Republic*, but it could be one of the imaginary exchanges Reagan recounted in order to retail his ideas to voters. Reagan, of course, would have provided his own, verbal, answers to the rhetorical questions he put to his audiences. Kersey answers with his gun.

Harry Callahan is a character whose essential nature is at odds with that of the reality in which he lives, while Paul Kersey is a character whose essential nature had been kept hidden from him by his benighted satisfaction with that reality. Both embody vague and anachronistic ideas about justice, both reach a point at which they feel obliged to say "fuck it" in connection with observing rules running counter to those ideas, except that in Harry's case the rules he chafes against are purely political (by contrast, his flippant disrespect toward "authority"—the Mayor,[10] the chief of police—is merely pro forma, meeting Hollywood prerequisites for a maverick hero; what places his career at risk is his principled disdain for "crazy" liberal laws), while for Kersey those rules are as devoid of *political* significance as his own putative liberalism.

While *Dirty Harry* directly challenges the way that the Constitution and the Bill of Rights are applied in the United States of America, *Death Wish* suggests an absence of enforcement, a systemic failure rather than a failure of design or interpretation. (That things don't work because they don't work—that jabberwocky of tautology, again—is precisely the narratological point.) Moreover, its primary philosophical stance is that the failure is to be located within contemporary "civilization"

---

10. Played by the ever-unctuous John Vernon.

itself. Here we move way beyond schematic questions of the law and its application and into the realm of will. *Dirty Harry* is full of citizens eager for the opportunity to do the right thing (Harry, surveilling a suspect, is beaten by a group of zealous civilians who believe he is a Peeping Tom); *Death Wish* is full of citizens eager only to crouch. The nightmare in *Dirty Harry* is the tolerance of bad laws; the nightmare in *Death Wish* is the tolerance of evil itself.

Where *Dirty Harry* draws doctrinaire conclusions—so much so that it's difficult to imagine undergoing a conversion in the theater if you enter feeling sanguine about Miranda and habeas corpus—*Death Wish* is more sinuous, postulating a what-if. What if this happened to you? What if, as Michael Dukakis was asked, someone raped and murdered your wife? What if there was an alternative, in place just across state lines, that worked? It has only to ask the questions to bring about uncomfortable self-reflection. I should mention that I am a liberal, a liberal who has been mugged, and I have remained one despite occasional inconsistencies of thought that worry me less than they reassure me that I am not an ideologue. Nevertheless, I'm generally in favor of all those patently liberal things that conservatives tend to deride—yet while I recoil at Sam's suggestion that the poor be relocated to concentration camps, I am not certain that Paul Kersey doesn't speak to me. It's useful to recall the responses after Bernhard Goetz—sometimes called "the *Death Wish* shooter" in the tabloids—shot four unarmed teenagers on a New York subway train late in 1984. Among the more notable, as reported in *Quiet Rage*, Lillian B. Rubin's study of the shootings: along the FDR Drive, someone graffitied POWER TO THE VIGILANTE! NY LOVES YA! and drivers reportedly honked their horns in agreement as they streamed past; Phil Donahue suggested on his show that Goetz was provoked by his fear of the sharpened screwdrivers the shooting victims were said to have brandished; Roy Innis, head of the Congress of Racial Equality, called Goetz "an avenger for all of us," and said of the undeniably racially tinged shootings, "Some black man ought to have done it long before . . . I wish it was me"; and Geoffrey Alpert, then director of the Center for the Study of Law and Society at the University of Miami, said, "This is . . . a story of human nature . . . It's something we'd all like to do. We'd all like to think we'd react the way he did." These responses took place in real time—as opposed to movie time—even as information casting the event in a more dubious light began to emerge: it was not clear if Goetz had actually been the victim of an attempted mugging. Apparently the screwdrivers were unsharpened, and were not brandished.

I suppose the purpose of this digression is to point out that, while the vicarious feelings we experience (whether we're willing to cop to them or not) are remarkably similar in either instance, there remains a universe of difference between infinitely complicated, not to say fucked up, events that take place in the world and tidy ones that we thrill to from our seats in a theater. Not being a narrative that allows for indeterminacy in any way (we see everything; in fact, as eyewitnesses to the attack on Joanna and Carol, we actually see far more than Paul, stuck at his office listening to Sam's

Winner shoots the rampaging of the Freaks at the supermarket as if it were a lost scene from *A Hard Day's Night.*

Space for life.

Media coverage
of the vigilante
punctuates
the film.

DW's rape and assault scene draws heavily on the home invasion depicted in *A Clockwork Orange*.

(continued on next two pages)

Hospital personnel, antiseptic in their white uniforms, ignore a man in need of help.

At the gun club, Paul Kersey is transformed.

Paul Kersey's scenes depict space to centrifugal effect, isolating him within crowds of people; while Inspector Ochoa's scenes are centripetal; with him always at the center of attention.

Kersey in his livingroom, the news report he is watching, and an omniscient depiction of the event being reported: the fictive horizon of the film begins to recede.

theories of social engineering), *Death Wish* closes off any possibility of extenuating nuance emerging to make Paul seem less righteous.[11] The nuance lies in our own answers to the questions the film raises, but since the film raises them in a mythic context, our answers are limited: the only valid responses are either to say "but of course" or to, in effect, walk out.

I could just say that this is the story of American narrative cinema in a nutshell and leave it at that. But to elaborate: writing on *Death Wish* in *The Myth of the American Superhero*, Lawrence and Jewett quote Richard Slotkin's *Regeneration Through Violence* on myth:

> A mythology is a complex of narratives that dramatizes the world vision and historical sense of a people or culture, reducing centuries of experience into a constellation of compelling metaphors . . . The believer's response to his myth is essentially nonrational and religious . . . he feels that the myth has put him in intimate contact with the ultimate powers which shape all of life . . . [providing] a scenario or prescription for action, defining and limiting the possibilities for human response to the universe.

Lawrence and Jewett then discuss three components comprising a "mythic paradigm" that drives the film, giving

---

11. Although, thanks to its four idiotic sequels (of which we are not obliged to say much), *Death Wish* does permit us a kind of insight that goes beyond the margins of the film: if we assume a continuum linking all five pictures, they gradually demonstrate that Paul Kersey is actually an unjustifiably bloodthirsty maniac.

it power despite what they call its "absurd images": *mythic selectivity* ("a process whereby an artifact defines the factual realities in a given situation"); *mythic massage* ("a process of assuring viewers that the gap between myth and reality can be bridged. In *Death Wish* . . . mythical redemption works out in everyday life according to mythical expectation"); and the *invitation to emulate:*

> Occasionally, [a film issues] a call that seems aimed at courageous viewers . . . In the case of *Death Wish*, the archetypal model of the Old West vigilante provides the invitation for responding to the modern urban situation. Kersey's modeling his behavior after a mythical paradigm suggests to the audience that they do likewise in becoming a superhero vigilante. The other option presented by the film is to remain an expectant but passive public waiting for salvation-by-vigilante. In the latter case, the public in the movie reinforces the spectator stance of the audience.

This "invitation" is precisely what makes some critics begin to sound bananas. Myth in pre-classical Thebes, or on the autochthonous Great Plains, or in 1881 Tombstone, apparently is one thing; myth in modern dress on location in twentieth-century Manhattan is another, more dangerous, thing. "Which American metropolis will have the honor of producing the first spin-off vigilante?" *Newsweek* worried.

But the myth is a closed system: it is as patently uninterested in the dangers of applying its "lessons" to the real world as it is in allowing the unknown quantities of reality into that system. Manipulative or not, the certitude of *Death Wish* is entirely justified by the history of storytelling itself. White hats and black hats have been around for a long time—hence the handy metonymy. And so have reviewers of various kinds telling us that certain stories shouldn't be told.

It's probably obvious by now that I reject the characterization of *Death Wish* as a propaganda film, although I think it does borrow certain conventions from the form—speeches that seem to pin a worldview to certain existing situations, grossly manipulative episodes, and demonstrations of the honor accruing to someone who subsumes his own interests under those of a righteous cause—none of which quite succeed in dissecting the situations, the relationships between the episodes and the decisions that seem to be made in their wake, or the nature of the cause. But it seems almost quaint to me that contemporary reviewers tried to locate a political agenda in a film that depicts its protagonist's embrace of a near-Hobbesian state of nature (that is, a pre-political state); this strikes me less as a response to the presence of political content in the film than as incomprehension in the face of violence depicted outside of accustomed cinematic contexts, although the extent of (and motivation for) such violence is identical to that found in more comfortably defined genre pictures of the time. Apparently, *Death Wish*'s essentially unironic approach to combining elements from those different genres and applying them to a scenario in a contemporary setting led to its being interpreted as a sincere and reprehensible prescription for contemporary problems. In 2010—an age of excruciatingly violent movies—

the tools exist for a more habituated reception of such films, and they're consequently met by a critical apparatus that casually concedes violence while discerning postmodern allusiveness as reflexively as it once did right-wing propaganda (e.g., the way that Quentin Tarantino is routinely criticized not for the violence in his films but for making films that are too "filmy"[12]). Still, the urge to see politics in *Death Wish* persists. Foster Hirsch, in *Detours and Lost Highways: A Map of Neo-Noir* (2004), sees in *Death Wish* a "skewed and reckless ideology" that "denies [Paul Kersey's] sickness." Peter Lev (*American Films of the 70s: Conflicting Visions*, 2000) sees "a right-wing perspective on the necessity of extralegal violence." In *The Suspense Thriller: Films in the Shadow of Alfred Hitchcock* (1988), Charles Derry detects "almost fascist sensibilities" in *Death Wish*. And so it goes.

I realize that it would be disingenuous of me to suggest that there's no correlation between what people line up to see at the

---

12. U.S. movie reviewers seem to possess an almost pragmatic blindness to the aesthetics of film, while remaining susceptible to all its manipulations. See David Denby's disapproving *New Yorker* review of *Inglourious Basterds*, in which he refers to the farmer who, at the outset of the film, is ultimately forced to give up the Jews he is hiding to the SS as "a man of great dignity." Even as Denby insists that he won't be fooled by Tarantino's metafictional shenanigans, he misses the point that the farmer's great dignity consists of the photography of his impassive but expressive face, his hands, his powerful body in repose; the business Tarantino has him do; the tear that rolls down his cheek—of his performance before Tarantino's cameras. Denby takes time out to honor a tar baby of "dignity" Tarantino assembled as if precisely for this purpose, but for Denby it is as if the character exists independently of Tarantino.

multiplex and the overall mood of the country, but the desire of a huge portion of the moviegoing public to watch people get shot to death has remained unchanged even as the country has staggered back and forth over the years across the center line dividing the political left and right. What one ultimately detects in the insistence on the presence of "fascism" or "far-right politics" or "sickness" within a film like *Death Wish* is a kind of shadow assertion that such things, latent in the unwashed audience, are urged forth from it by such films.

Emotionally, this may be the case, but it isn't politics. It is more akin to what Roland Barthes describes in "The World of Wrestling" as "the perfect intelligibility of reality," brought about by action that "discards all parasitic meanings and ceremonially offers to the public a pure and full signification, rounded like Nature . . . an ideal understanding of things; it is the euphoria of men raised for a while above the constitutive ambiguity of everyday situations."

3

Death Wish and Performance

Hope Lange

It's a "thankless role," but Hope Lange manages to do a lot with it. Joanna Kersey is a middle-aged woman with a grown and married child, loved by her husband but still somewhat at loose ends. Until the moment at the supermarket when it becomes clear what is going to happen, the film could easily have been about her, one of the many movies made in the 1970s about middle-aged women arriving at a crossroads of purpose. Paul could make that trip to Tucson and meet a beautiful young developer—played by Jill Ireland, perhaps—and deliver the news of his own particular fork in the road to Joanna from a motel phone. But a film about a woman savagely murdered while attempting to make her own life would have been too cruel—we would look forward to *Mr. Goodbar* for that. There's the echo present in the movie of actorly, and perhaps even womanly, determination to make the most of a small and frankly difficult—Lange spends half of her screen time being menaced and beaten—role. Before that she manages to convey traces of exhibitionism—what remains of the desire to display a beautiful body—and coy self-deprecation. When Paul tells her that she has a "prime figure," she tells him, "That's a euphemism for fat," but she knows it isn't, and she knows that she isn't fat. It's difficult, I imagine, to be a woman in her position: to look fine, but not young; to be open to arousal, but not salaciousness. To be better looking and more attractive than your own daughter.

What's different about this role is the degree to which it is body-centric. We see Lange in her bathing suit, talking about having sex on a beach, then see her body being violated with fists, blackjacks, feet. (The similarly difficult job of Janet Leigh in *Psycho* comes to mind—in both instances there's a definite, corporeal sense of something going to waste.[13])

There's reason and exasperation here. Lange gives us one face for the beach—the "uncivilized" face of radiant joy and sexual response—and another for sitting in taxis, paying at the checkout stand, dealing with violent predators. It's an interesting and nuanced performance—just watch the smirk of self-indulgent superiority at the Hawaiian restaurant while the "native dancers" twitch, virtually the only sign in the film that the "Hawaii" of this instantiation is not to be believed in, is strictly for the tourists; the little flutter of frustration, so familiar as to be almost imperceptible, in the stranded taxicab, the exhaustion of that fifteen-hour journey in the restrained exasperation of her body language as Paul checks the mail in the lobby of their building: she's thinking, "He can never

---

13. In *Bronson's Loose!: The Making of the* Death Wish *Films*, Paul Talbot writes that Winner suggested that Jill Ireland be cast in the role of Joanna Kersey, but that Bronson refused the suggestion, not wanting his wife to be subjected to such on-screen brutalization.

just let it go!" There's a definite sense here that, despite his lustful suggestion on the beach, it's not Joanna who's too civilized, but Paul. Yet obligations to a husband, a household, a daughter who insists on coming over to inspect the souvenir tchotchkes even before they've unpacked—these make us "civilized" whether we want to be or not.

So in a sense Lange sets us up to see the far side of her Hawaiian yearning when she encounters the opposite of civilization right in her own living room. In the one scene in which Winner shows real interest in montage, he gives us a lot of her. The camera checks in with her to share her reaction after we have seen what is going on in the room; the actors playing the thugs mug and writhe, but ultimately, at least on repeated viewings, we watch her: smoothing her clothes after Jeff Goldblum releases her, keeping her face composed even as it radiates terror, surrendering finally to horror—a fairly brilliant piece of acting.

Kathleen Tolan

On the other hand, some actors succumb to their roles as props. Kathleen Tolan seems aware that she is there to be photographed, first like a meal, and then like a meal being eaten, and there's a primness to her, as if her knowledge of the way the story will unfold—that she will end up half-naked and simulating oral copulation—has decided her on approaching the role as if she were playing a librarian or a pedantic schoolmarm in an antediluvian comedy. Just watch that stiff walk from the bedroom to the front door; it could have been accompanied by a Sousa march. The problem is that the scene of the assault is so completely overstated, with the "freaks" announcing what they plan to do and narrating it while they do it (all the thugs in the movie are chatty), that the contrast between a woman who is put together and a woman who is torn apart becomes equally overstated: to be put together doesn't necessarily mean to be as tightly wound as a mechanical toy, and played as such she comes off as manifestly unpleasant: while Joanna chats familiarly with the checkout girl at the supermarket, Carol gives her a frozen smile and a glassy stare that we catch a glimpse of as she turns to go. Carol's in a kind of coma long before the movie maneuvers her into one; or perhaps she's just one of those people who feel it necessary to be unpleasant to those she considers her social inferiors. Certainly her husband, Jack, gives the impression of being terminally henpecked.

She speaks four lines: "Bye," "I'll get it," "Who is it?" and "No!"

William Redfield

William Redfield was a ubiquitous actor during this period, or at least he seemed to be everywhere, and he was such a familiar face that I remember feeling a sense of loss when I found out he'd died, at forty-nine, of leukemia. As Sam, Redfield makes a thoroughly unpleasant character—posturing in human dress—palatable; his downtrodden everyman appearance makes the obnoxious lines he's given to speak seem redolent of cowardly fearfulness (fascism's best friend, as Roosevelt cunningly reminded us when he was inaugurated as president a month after Hitler became German chancellor) rather than ideological conviction. In his jittery bonhomie—chattering uneasily at his own cocktail party, diffidently asking Paul if he'll see him for lunch—he does seem like that nice-enough guy from the office, mired somewhere in middle management, the one who will either share with you his ideas about the camps or show you the Polaroids exhaustively documenting his home renovation project.

Chris Gampel

Another office type, hale and hearty. *Death Wish* does a fair job of sketching the ghost outlines of a comedy of manners, locating many of its attitudes around the water cooler. You can imagine much of the supporting cast sustaining one of those stagey dark comedies, a group of average people of above-average means maneuvering through their lives and the urban landscape while an unknown vigilante dominates the headlines. Muriel Spark might have written the script.

But Chris Gampel is so healthy-looking—when he tells Paul that "Tucson agreed with you . . . You look well," he himself looks as if he's just flown in on the Learjet from Sun Valley—and wears his authority so lightly that you almost forget that he spends most of his time in the movie giving Charles Bronson orders.

Steven Keats

The first thing I think of, when I think of Steven Keats, is the scene in *The Friends of Eddie Coyle* when Robert Mitchum's Eddie explains to Keats's gun dealer how he got an extra set of knuckles. This is just by way of noting how some big, handsome actors who look as if they were born to tread the boards and be admired from Row 40 end up in the shadow of overwhelming screen presences. So it goes here, with virtually all of Keats's scenes played with Bronson. Jack Toby looks like one of those peculiar Disney hybrid characters, the upright creatures with sculpted haircuts and the faces of dogs. Jack whines and looks helpless when he fills Kersey (and us) in on what's going on with Carol; his information is almost always incomplete. Unlike his model in the source novel—a dyed-in-the-wool liberal and Legal Aid Society lawyer who lectures Paul about due process—he seems simply like the sort of schlub Nassau County was built to house; everything about him says that the most seductive thing anyone could ever whisper in his ear is "Great Neck." Keats reads his lines with mechanical emphasis, almost as if he learned them phonetically or, possibly, is registering dismay with the role. The problem is that, having written him in for Bronson to bounce dialogue off, both Keats and the movie seem at a loss as to what to do with him otherwise.

Stuart Margolin

Stuart Margolin is the only actor in the film who actually pushes Bronson to the margins of our attention. He manages this without upstaging Bronson in any way; in fact, he permits Bronson to draw on his own immense presence without seeming to be posing. Margolin plays Ames Jainchill from the waist, with movement radiating upward to his arms, gesturing, resting on a surface, or wrapped around his midsection; and downward to his legs, which strut and saunter. He's a bantam, but Margolin uses his head sparingly, in concert with his entire body, a nice lesson for a hundred better-known actors who play cocky and assertive guys from the neck up, the body trailing helplessly behind the aggressive movement of the head—amazing how often a George Clooney or a Tom Cruise, at least in early roles, has looked as if he is miming being punched in the face while delivering his lines. Ames talks a lot, but Margolin turns him into a physical presence, and Bronson responds beautifully, generally anchoring the frame in relative stillness while Margolin struts and gestures around him.

We first see him as he pushes through the swinging doors of a Western saloon—an airport cocktail lounge. With Margolin, the film actually seems to be having a good time with its references. The script tells us the West is real, Margolin and the film tell us the West is fake—a contradiction that matters not at all: let's drink, let's eat, let's shoot our guns here in Old Tucson, it's all dumb fun. Ames gives us the feeling that New York's biggest problem might be in taking things too seriously; the huge gaps in Ames's philosophy that the narrative must span—linking money-grubbing to a "toilet" of a city to gun control—Margolin bridges effortlessly, just by making us want to be with him. Ames serves Vladimir Propp's function of the "magical donor" in the narrative, but what could have been a humorless errand of acquisition becomes a joyous interlude, the gun he provides a souvenir of particular usefulness.

Vincent Gardenia

Inspector Frank Ochoa possesses a kind of amused authority, whether dealing with subordinates or superiors. When he utters the line "I just wanted to hear you say it" to the district attorney—who's admitted that he doesn't want to apprehend Paul Kersey because he fears making a "martyr" of him—he says it like a man who doesn't want to hear you say anything that disagrees with him or doesn't confirm his suspicions. (It's a good interpretation of the basic cop persona.) Gardenia can't really shed the donnish patriarch that reposes in his blunt physicality. Every question is a rhetorical snare, every speech a lesson, perhaps a moral one, notwithstanding the fact that he ultimately comes off as a man who has resigned himself to abusing his personal standards for reasons of professional pragmatism. If the game takes place in a constantly shifting political and media environment, then OK, the nature of winning it honorably changes as well. I mention this because Gardenia manages to retain the aura of salt-of-the-earth virtue even after the movie has made it plain that his every act is going to have to be a kind of self-betrayal. He pulls off the neat trick of holding suspended in a mutually inimical space both a sense of that virtue and a vested interest in an inspector's pension.

The rank of inspector, by the way, is actually a pretty senior one within the NYPD, not subject to its own qualifying civil service exam and conferred at the discretion of the commissioner. Which is to say that it's unlikely one would be summoned to the scene when a junkie ex-con is discovered murdered in Riverside Park. This is probably partly a cultural mistranslation; in Winner's Britain a detective inspector would have been placed in charge of an investigation. On the other hand, Ochoa was conceived a little differently. He couldn't be that police lieutenant we've seen in a million movies, the desk-bound centaur—half man, half swivel chair—continually bowing to unspecified political pressures from a metonymic "tenth floor," saying, "Listen up, people," dressing down his rogue star detective, collecting badge and gun from same; that long-annealed, long-suffering persona, a bureaucrat designed to stifle violent genius. Ochoa is born to run things—as, indeed, Gardenia runs his portion of the film—from his position between the high brass and the rank-and-file, conveying an indulgent and familiar sense of institutional politics that precludes true disgust: I'm tempted to say that it makes sense that it took a native Neapolitan actor to pull this off so convincingly. To Ochoa, everyone's cut from the same cloth: Halting an underling's rude interrogation of a mugging victim who insists that he hasn't seen Kersey's face, Ochoa smiles and sucks on his cigar. "You sawr him pretty good, dincha?" When the man vehemently shakes his head, Ochoa bares his teeth in a smile of genuine pleasure at the predictability of human nature: "You're fulla shit."

Gardenia makes a lot of room for himself in the movie—befitting *Death Wish*'s awkward lurch at the halfway mark, when it breaks its rhythm to shift from Paul Kersey's exclusive story to a cat-and-mouse game, involving aspects of a police procedural, between two characters with irreconcilable goals. He plays his role sniffling, sneezing, wheezing, sucking on an inhaler, then lighting a cigar, spraying Binaca, and starting the cycle again. The hamminess of the performance is canny—Frank Ochoa is becoming a media star, after all, with his mug on the cover of *People*—but beneath it is the discernment that a line supervisor is always a kind of beleaguered schoolteacher.

To a section of this book filled with digressive speculation, I'll add that it would have been a far better idea than a series of *Death Wish* sequels to spin Ochoa off into his own TV program, perhaps on the old *NBC Sunday Mystery Movie*.

Stephen Elliott

One day I was having breakfast at my parents' house in Palo Alto when my mother pointed out a picture of George Shultz, then the secretary of state, on the front page of the *Times*: "Look at him," she said, "sleek as a seal." She tendered this with a kind of sneaking admiration; I think that like a lot of people my mother has always appreciated those who enjoy their privilege, regardless of their politics. Stephen Elliott made a career out of playing military officers, judges, physicians, and tycoons, particularly on film, mostly because of that seal-like sleekness, which gave him the air of slightly unctuous gravitas. As the police commissioner he is charged perfectly with the task of telling lies in public and ordering others to tell lies in private.

Freaks

I've already described the scene at the supermarket as something out of *A Hard Day's Night*. I wrote it offhand, but then remembered that before Stanley Kubrick bought the rights to the project, the Rolling Stones were interested in acquiring *A Clockwork Orange* and casting themselves as Alex and the Droogs. Is it really too much of a stretch to consider the possibility of being mugged by the Beatles? History is murky on this point, but members of the group apparently did engage in destructively antisocial behavior during their Hamburg residencies, and the violence of John Lennon, at least, is well documented. And the group did, after all, take the name of the "bad" motorcycle gang in *The Wild One*. All of which is to say that Winner's impulse (actually Kubrick's impulse, but more on that later) to render mindless violence as a kind of radiant and liberating joy goes way back to the process of identifying the energy that permitted the modification of the hard-rocking, pill-popping Beatles into the pillow-fighting, cavorting Fab Four—not the total transformation people have claimed it is, but a more subtle shifting of certain emphases—and restoring its proper outlet.

The only criminals we get to know are Freak #1, Freak #2, and Spraycan Freak (Jeff Goldblum, Christopher Logan, and Gregory Rozakis, respectively). Are there actually "performances" here? I suppose technically, although really all the attackers in the film are there to fill the screen with a certain kind of sound and fury, and then run, or fall; and in any case thirty-six years later we find ourselves waiting expectantly for the appearance of Goldblum, bedecked ridiculously with Jughead Jones's hat. Far more menacing is the performance by the uncredited actor playing the role of the first mugger Kersey shoots, who exudes a slimy desperation perfectly captured in the rare close-up Winner grants him.

Charles Bronson

He wasn't really working with a lot of range, but he'd learned to use that body of his, and that face, mostly how to keep them still, bestowing implication when either moved, and a sense of fulfillment when they moved forcefully. The promise of violence never seemed far from Bronson—hence the ridicule with which many critics greeted his having been cast in *Death Wish* as both a liberal and white-collar professional. Such ridicule doesn't matter much, since it doesn't shed light on either the movie or on the performance, but only on the reviewers' aptitude as spectators; what they "know," as if the rest of us don't. (Barthes on wrestlers, again: they "have a physique as peremptory as those of the characters of the Commedia dell'Arte, who display in advance, in their costumes and attitudes, the future contents of their parts.") So it went with Bronson; what had kept this in check, or below the radar, was his long career as a featured (though often monosyllabic and brutish) player in ensemble pictures with other actors whose particular virility was equally "peremptory": Steve McQueen, Yul Brynner, Lee Marvin, James Coburn, etc. There's nothing especially "wrong" with this; very few stars are truly protean, and those who are often paradoxically end up being mundane in their versatility (see Philip Seymour Hoffman). In any case, while the point wasn't to cast Bronson as a believable engineer, but as a believable bearer of death, Bronson is not misplaced in either mode. I mentioned earlier that at the turning point in the film Paul Kersey becomes "Charles Bronson"; once you stop hurrying through the movie to see what happens and begin watching it to see the way that it happens, this metamorphosis becomes clear. One of Winner's most effective scenes is the one set at the shooting range in Tucson, where Bronson's physical attitude gradually shifts from hand-fluttering discomfort, even disorientation, to an authoritative familiarity. Winner ends the scene with a close-up of Bronson's hand holding a Colt single-action revolver as he expertly cocks it.

Death Wish does a lot of noisy and provocative yammering, but Bronson moves outside the bubble of the film's rhetoric, moves, like Melville's ironically recounted "Indian-hater," outside the bubble of the film's world, freed at last to be his own context. You sense that he has discovered a tremendous solitariness inside himself, a need for that beyond the simpler need of vengeance. Was it always so? Again, the quixotic impulse to see past the frame: Hope Lange's performance surely intimates a certain dissatisfaction; for that there must be a corollary. Is this terrible freedom what Kersey has been waiting for?

Certainly it was the role and setting that Bronson had been waiting for. Movies like *The Great Escape* and *The Magnificent Seven* force their characters into dependence on loyalty and esprit de corps, qualities such films sometimes suggest are alien to them and that are, to be sure, tested in furtherance of a specific goal. Even Bronson's solo starring roles that deal specifically with themes of revenge are ad hoc. But Paul Kersey—curiously, when you think about it—doesn't seek out the three "freaks" who have destroyed his family. He undertakes a principled commitment to an abstract concept of perpetual revenge. For Paul Kersey the silence, the stillness, the secrecy, will be continuous, and Bronson does not portray him as a man in torment, but as a man rejuvenated.

Bronson would go on to give better performances—including one the next year as an itinerant and enigmatic boxer in

Hard Times—but this one made him a big star in the United States, cementing his screen persona and destroying him as an actor. I exaggerate: with Winner (and others) he already had collaborated in eroding the quality of remote secrecy promised by his inscrutably hewn face, leaving only the known quantity of efficient violence. That violence could be vengeful (*Chato's Land*), mercenary (*The Mechanic*), or simply sadistic (*The Stone Killer*) in nature, and I suppose that the potential for it was the thing we suspected of him all along, but with *Death Wish* the fever actually began to break, violence withdrawing behind the shell of civility (or order) and awaiting means, motive, and opportunity to emerge. It didn't matter: the film was too big a hit; and perhaps because it had so thoroughly desublimated his onscreen presence he was never as useful or effective again: everything afterward was to be a restatement of his own revealed subtext. The role of the pitiless killer became the one he all-too-readily embraced, even as Hollywood (as exemplified by the grind-house aesthetic of the Cannon Group) transformed pitilessness first into psychopathy and then into the model of the Killing Machine, which today can be seen operating smoothly in the guise of actors ranging from Matt Damon to Liam Neeson to Daniel Craig to Bruce Willis. Bronson's later filmography is almost entirely meretricious stuff, breathtakingly brutal gun porn, and he retired from the screen after *Death Wish V: The Face of Death*, well into his seventies and visibly tired from schlepping around the increasingly large arsenal, ultimately including rocket launchers and the M60 machine gun, with which he dispatched ever greater numbers of evildoers. Someone has done us all the favor of compiling an anthology of every gunshot fired in each of the five *Death Wish* films, more or less obviating the need to actually view the later films. The clip (available in two parts on YouTube) runs approximately fourteen minutes.

4

Death Wish as Film

In *Bronson's Loose!* Paul Talbot writes that Michael Winner "chooses his camera angles on the spot, rarely does more than two takes, and shoots very little extraneous footage." Winner is quoted as saying, "I make it up on the day." One consequence of this manner of working is that you can tell which scenes in *Death Wish* bored him. A more formally rigorous approach might have enabled Winner to generate interest from scenes that lay flat in the shooting script (or to eliminate them), and more concern for what was happening before his cameras might have allowed him more frequently to capture performances, rather than the antic blocking that occupies so much of the film. But his method does let us see clearly which sequences he deemed worth lavishing attention on, which effects he attempted deliberately to achieve, what influences came into play.

Some general notes on the film's overall look: With notable exceptions, cutting is kept to a minimum, with many scenes built around what in a different context would be the master shot encompassing all the actors. Winner's camera sometimes anticipates the actors' movements, other times tracks around still figures; or he will station the camera in one position, panning as the actors move across the frame or enter it to approach their marks. Cutting only occasionally entails the typical shot-reverse-shot strategy; instead Winner often favors lingering reaction shots in which one of the characters is seen absorbing what he's just seen or heard. Transitions between scenes are accomplished entirely by direct cuts, with no fades or dissolves, and many scenes begin with a door opening to reveal one or more of the characters, or with a close-up of a small object or feature of a space from which the camera pulls back or reverse zooms to reveal the larger scene. The film is mostly shot in deep focus with a wide-angle lens—so wide that barrel distortion occurs at the edges of the frame, the straight lines and right angles of interiors appearing bowed—with Winner often placing the actors in the center of the frame, using medium shots so that we see as much as possible of what is around them (an interesting echo of Ames Jainchill's complaint about profit-driven developers' seeking to eliminate "wasted space"; what might have been a more conventionally dynamic and tighter movie, certainly by today's rapid-cut standards, becomes one of almost languorous patience).

The issue is with the payoff. Small gems are revealed on repeated viewings—e.g., one picture on Paul Kersey's living room wall is a Picasso reproduction depicting Don Quixote, another self-styled knight-errant modeling his behavior on a romantic notion of the past—but while there are some scenes in which the "noise" inhabiting the different planes of the image is of crucial interest (e.g., at the hospital to which Joanna and Carol are brought after the attack), some where it halfheartedly pretends to documentary realism (the police station, the coffee shop), and some where a spurious faux symbolism threatens to carry the movie off the rails (the repeated appearance of nuns,[14] the dwarf newsman), for the most part the frame is filled with vast amounts of banal information that lends neither color nor texture.

A key influence on the picture is Stanley Kubrick, an influence explicitly acknowledged in the scene depicting the assault at the Kersey apartment, which quotes directly from the notorious "Singin' in the Rain" episode from *A Clockwork Orange*, and in the shot of Paul Kersey gyrating wildly with the sock weighted with rolls of quarters after having used it successfully to beat off a mugger, which recalls the hominid's victory dance with the bone he has learned to use as a weapon in the opening sequence of *2001: A Space Odyssey*. Although Kubrick's methodical approach is as far from Winner's "make it up on the day" attitude as can be imagined, his visual sensibility pervades the movie in its wide angles, large depth of field, uncomfortably lingering shots, and tracking of characters down corridors. Like Kubrick, Winner is fascinated with institutions—supermarkets, hospitals, banks, airline terminals, police precinct houses, subway stations, offices—public and semi-public spaces whose sterility, squalor, or grandeur contrasts with or complements the appearance and demeanor

---

14. Brian Garfield tells Talbot an amusing anecdote: "I asked Winner, 'What's with the three nuns?' He replied, 'They're symbols, dear boy.' I said, 'Symbolizing what?' He replied, 'Nothing, darling, they're just symbols.' I got the feeling we were living through a cheap imitation of Fellini."

of the actors, and there's a leisurely studiousness to the depiction of such settings. But since Winner possesses neither Kubrick's perverse (even infantile) sense of humor nor his meticulousness, he's not always sure what to do with them: sometimes, the best he can come up with is a kind of half-assed irony (the scene at JFK that begins with a close-up of a picture-postcard of Manhattan on which the phrase "Glittering New York" is printed), or the kind of mugging and cavorting that he has the three "freaks" do. Winner also lacks Kubrick's autistic concentration, the urge to focus on an object or mise-en-scène that goes beyond contemplation and into fixation. There's a kind of glibness to the entire production, a glibness that sometimes works—as when Winner is putting together his simplified and schematic New York—but that at other times undercuts even the film's most serious intentions. More crucially, Winner creates very few images of true beauty in *Death Wish*, and while you understand that the camera is an undiscriminating machine, you wonder why Winner has to be.

It's too bad, because there's definite evidence here of method undone by both impatience and condescension: the whore at the coffee shop picks her nose *and* ostentatiously widens her eyes at the sight of Bronson's wad of cash? Please. What is apparent enough in context all too often is made blatantly obvious.

(And what about such abrupt, seemingly expedient point-of-view shifts? We can forgive the shift from Kersey to show the attack on Joanna and Carol, a manipulation of our feelings so brazen that it becomes admirable—Raymond Durgnat, writing on *Psycho*, speaks of its "emotionalisation of a *sufficiently typical* 'target audience,'" a characterization that suits this particular diegetic bypass in *Death Wish*—but do we need to see things from the point of view of the "freaks"? Of the subway car muggers? Of the muggers [and the whore] in the coffee shop? That kind of promiscuity often is called for in a narrative, but *Death Wish* very deliberately sticks close to Kersey until the second half of the film, where it begins to alternate between Kersey's and Ochoa's points of view, and even after that the intrusion of the perspectives of others corrupts what is otherwise a thoughtful purity to the dialectical tension that exists between these two characters.)

Where does *Death Wish* work, or at least work hard, as film? A lot of the movie was just a matter of putting people in front of a camera and filming them, thereby defying analysis, but I'll try to identify the key scenes and sequences from which an overall methodology and set of internal rules begin to emerge, and where the exceptions to those rules are deliberate and effective.

"Put them in concentration camps."

Our first look at Paul Kersey's office and our only real glimpse of the everyday life that subsequent events are about to undermine. We begin with a close-up of a dot-matrix printer generating reports on the money-losing Jainchill development; the camera zooms out to show us the surrounding action, Kersey removing the reports from the printer while Sam harangues him. This is both a precise way of opening a scene (printer=office; certainly the case in 1974), and mildly disorienting (where are we, who's here?). Sam fills Paul in on the rampant criminal activity in New York during his absence, launching into what seems like a well-polished spiel about the "underprivileged" and their rightful place (i.e., concentration camps). Paul appears to tolerate Sam, who tags along with him as the camera first follows, then leads, as the two stroll through the office suite, which is filled with architectural drawings and models whose own three-dimensional perspective becomes an extension of the filmic space—a nice conceit. In one particularly witty shot, Kersey, Sam, and their boss, Ives, are grouped at the foot of a scale model of Manhattan Island, looming like enormous idols, the first of several instances in which Winner uses the set dressing to create odd juxtapositions with his actors.

"Would you have these delivered, please, Mary?"
At the supermarket where Joanna Kersey and Carol Toby go shopping, the colors are almost as eye-popping as in Hawaii. The entire scene is a kind of info dump, filled with noise and static and possessing the most facile kind of Pop Art sensibility: All that abundance! All those colorfully familiar brands and displays! The Muzak, placid and saccharine even as Fate fingers the Kersey women for their doom! Oh, "civilization," how blind and feckless you are! The Kerseys eat a lot of processed grains, by the way. Corn Chex, Mister Salty pretzels, and Quaker cereal.

Again, Winner opens with a close-up of a machine—a cash register—before zooming back to show the larger picture.

This inaugurates the series of public scenes in the film, and is the first time that Winner directs his actors to move obliviously and dreamily through the frame—given the behavior of the "freaks" that they are seemingly unaware of, or pretending not to notice, it implicates "the public" in a kind of apathy that carries forward through the remaining public sequences taking place in New York and contrasts with the attentive and strongly responsive "public" witnessing the gunfight in Old Tucson.

"I'm gonna paint her mouth."

The attack at the Kersey apartment. The influence of *A Clockwork Orange* on this scene would be hard to overstate. Kubrick's mean-spiritedness (the victims, and the fussy minimalism of their home, are ripe for violation at the hands of Alex and his Droogs; the violence of the scene, the implicit comeuppance it embodies, are close to what the Marx Brothers loosed upon their supercilious foils) places his own rape-and-assault scene perfectly in the middle of a two-hour-and-twenty-minute moral argument so schematic as to represent a void (it is not one of my favorites among the great director's films), and his willingness to carry much further than necessary the not-particularly-funny joke of Malcolm McDowell accompanying his acts of battery, vandalism, and rape with a rendition of "Singin' in the Rain" demands that we laugh, if not at the depicted events then at the director's willful excesses. Still, Kubrick's scene works, perhaps, because it provides the opportunity for McDowell to apotheosize both Alex's physical essence and his bored intelligence, especially contrasted with that of his Droogs (*vide* Dim's moronic echolalia). But who are *Death Wish*'s "freaks," really, other than a trio of hyperkinetic (and verbose) plot devices? "I kill rich cunts." "I'm gonna stiff you in the ass." "Mother's getting the shit kicked out of her." "I'm gonna paint her mouth." If Kubrick leaves us with the peculiar choice of either laughing or recoiling in disgust (both responses are equally plausible), Winner is simply blunt, try as he might (and he does try) to be otherwise: over more than sixty cuts (Kubrick, ever patient, makes fewer than twenty-five in a scene of nearly exactly the same length) the camera moves, the camera remains still, the camera staggers, handheld, the camera finally rises from the level of the floor. Winner uses some of the extreme close-ups that he doles out so sparingly here, alternating shots of Joanna's bloodied face with POV shots of the freaks sexually abusing her daughter.

"There's a man over there, he's bleeding. And nobody comes."

At the hospital. Among the most careful scenes in the film. Again Winner begins with a close-up, this time of a distorting mirror in which we spy Kersey's reflection as he heads up the hospital corridor. The setting is a hospital, but really it's one of sharp angles; vertical, horizontal, and diagonal planes carved out of light and shadow. When Kersey and Jack Toby withdraw into an alcove to wait for news of Joanna and Carol, the camera films them from behind two panes of glass, the vertical line of the window frame dividing the picture in two, as well as dividing the two men from each other. Again we have an instance in which extras parade through the scene, now ghostly and antiseptic in their white uniforms; again, there are contrasting figures on the scene: Kersey, Toby, a policeman in his dark-blue uniform, and, most strikingly, a bloodied man, standing alone in the middle of the white room as hospital personnel sweep past him: Is he the figure in a nightmare, or is the staff's uncaring obliviousness to his condition the nightmare he's having? When Kersey tries to attract the attention of a nurse, she brushes him off, then disappears up one of the endless arterial corridors leading to and from this place; we're made to feel the familiar sensation that a hospital waiting room is the still center of uncaring.

"The good news of life beyond life."

Joanna's funeral. As the studious-looking minister piously intones the words of cold comfort over the grave of the newly deceased murder victim, you can just feel that uniquely British amused rancor toward religious hypocrisy. Hitchcock, of course, was the classic purveyor of such impiety (the next year he would, in his final film, play the kidnapping of a bishop for laughs). Does it have a place in what "should be" a sober scene? Maybe I'm only imagining it, because what I can't really imagine is that the minister's words here are words that could comfort me. (Perhaps I should note that in Brian Garfield's book, "Paul Benjamin" is Jewish.) There's something to be said about color here, I suppose—the sterile white, recalling the previous scene at the hospital, falling from the sky onto the morose dark mourning worn by everyone present—though I really want to note that the centrifugal motif of crowds of people orbiting around Paul Kersey, never engaging him, is especially apparent:

even at his wife's funeral, he is an anonymous figure in the midst of a crowd; no one approaches or talks to the little family group consisting of Paul, Jack, and Carol; Sam is referred to but, although William Redfield is clearly visible following Bronson to the limousine, he does not speak. Weirdly, Sam and three other mourners who appear to be waiting for Paul (who has said that he will be traveling back to New York with them) disappear completely in the moment Paul turns to look back at Joanna's grave—he is left mysteriously isolated in the snowbound cemetery: loneliness in a crowd always, even if the crowd is focused on his own sorrow.

Tucson, Old and New

An important sequence, and one of the film's inspired diegetic improvements on the source novel. Brian Garfield hustles Paul Benjamin out to Tucson in order to have him buy a gun, and also to get laid—it's hard to tell which is more important. Throughout, his Paul thinks of Tucson in the most condescending terms: "Cowboy boots went thudding past; he looked up at the receding shape of a big man in a business suit and a white ten-gallon hat. He had an urge to snicker. The man in boots and hat left the place and Paul swept his glance along the bar, the people at the bar. They were all so anxious that strangers should like their desert city. The forced hospitality, the desperate boosterism." I don't cite this to fault the opinions Garfield provides Paul; they're accurate enough representations of what someone from a genuinely cosmopolitan cultural center might be likely to think of a provincial one. But Garfield might as well have sent Paul to North Carolina, since for the book's purposes he's there only to obtain a pistol. Winner blends the West's gun-packing ethos with its own encoded myths, backing gently into self-reflexivity, sometimes baldly ("They shoot movies here sometimes," one movie actor, Stuart Margolin, says to another, Charles Bronson; the poster for Winner's *Lawman* hanging on the wall at the gun club), sometimes subtly (Kersey's work on the Jainchill development, reinforcing his own absorption of those myths, is an impressionistic filmic collage—twenty-seven cuts in forty-five seconds—that compresses time in order to convey progress in precisely the manner of a million Western films depicting hard work as a rite of passage that transforms the effete Eastern tenderfoot). The result is a deeply enhanced sense of the legitimacy of "Tucson" and the idea it embodies, not Garfield's let-me-get-my-gun-and-get-the-hell-out-of-here. Or perhaps "legitimacy" isn't the word: here, Winner continually plays with the idea of the fake, of the nostalgic. We first see Jainchill exiting a saloon through its swinging doors, but that saloon is in an airport terminal. In Old Tucson, a gunfight is presented as an event staged for the appreciation of spectators, a play-within-the-film that's to be repeated later, when Paul watches television-news stories about "ordinary citizens" who have followed his example to take the law into their own hands. At the gun club, the weapons Kersey fires are not the contemporary weapons carried by apparently almost everyone in Tucson, but antiques, one of which belonged to a gunfighter of the 1890s, "Candy Dan." (Even the pistol Jainchill gives Paul, a Colt Police Positive revolver, is an obsolescent weapon, first introduced in 1907.)

It's during Paul's first visit to the development site, and then at Jainchill's office, that we begin to realize how important Jainchill is to the entire sequence. At the site, the camera is planted at a distance from the two actors, who occupy positions on the left and right sides of the frame, twinned hills behind them. In the office, Paul is in the center of the frame, standing gigantically over a scale model of Jainchill's "wasteful" development (as he had stood earlier over a scale model of "efficient" Manhattan). In both scenes, Paul remains relatively still while Jainchill moves and lectures: he is indoctrinating Paul.

This reverses, literally, during the scene at the gun club. While Jainchill pontificates, the camera moves closer: first Jainchill on the left, Bronson on the right; then tight on Bronson, now tight on Jainchill; then, from far out on the range, their positions are reversed, a closer shot from the same vantage, then tight on Jainchill, now tight on Bronson. It's a wonderful, rhythmic ballet, not a subjective shot-reverse-shot separation, but more as if we are looking from character to character, trying to determine who holds the authority. In what I think is the most thrilling shot in the film—thrilling, maybe, because it so eloquently provides evidence of intelligent life behind the camera—we make our determination: after Bronson has fired a pistol for the first time "in a long time," he tells the story of his history with guns, and his decision to abandon them. The camera, shooting at first from behind Jainchill, slowly carries us over to Bronson's side of the frame, reversing the point of view. Emotionally, our determination is made easily: Bronson has the same facility with guns as Jainchill, his reason for abandoning them is principled and understandable, and we alone—he never mentions Joanna and Carol to Jainchill—know why he has picked one up again. The scene is Bronson's after this. A subsequent close-up of Jainchill shows him in silence, for the first time.

"To Paul, From Ames"

Back in his apartment, after having received the news from Jack, not of "life beyond life," but that Carol is "almost a goddamned vegetable" (in a scene that Winner, apparently bored, shoots from inside Eero Saarinen's TWA terminal as if it were a barn[15]), we see Paul looking exactly like what the movie has managed to avoid showing him as: a tired and lonely middle-aged man. It's as if this aspect of his character floods him at this moment, a good one for Bronson, under-stated—less is always more for him, and Winner is often at his best when no one's talking (he becomes interested then in what the camera is actually showing). Paul examines the Hawaiian vacation photos that have just arrived in the mail, and then unwraps the gift Jainchill has given him; Herbie Hancock's love theme building to a Liberace-like crescendo and then segueing into the hammer-strike chords of his gun theme when Paul lifts the .32 from its case and turns it over

15. I don't mean to insist on the cinematographic fetishization of "signifi-cant" architecture, but the film does, after all, deal with space and people's relationship to it, and toward one another within it. Winner appears to be trying to assimilate the space, to diminish it—the most perversely admirable thing about the scene is the way that he seemingly ferrets out every right angle in this famously curvaceous interior to frame it in his accustomed manner.

in his large hands. A nice subjective shot puts the gun in our own hands.

"I'll bust you up."
The first killing. A lot of people did get irritated by *Death Wish*'s depiction of the seeming ease with which one could be victimized in New York; they have their point, but I would argue (again) against confusing the film's mythic naturalism with an attempt at realism, and, to be fair, any movie does have a need to compress events, something Inspector Ochoa alludes to later when he suggests that Paul might have been schlepping around his grocery bag of gingersnaps and sugar, waiting to be mugged, for hours. But, for the record: Paul is stalked by a mugger within twenty-two seconds of setting foot in Riverside Park.

Winner does have a way with a close-up. The relative rarity of his use of them can sometimes make them seem as random and jarring as the things real life forces us to look at.[16] Here we have the paired close-ups of the mugger's face—oily, desperate, acne-pitted—and Paul's, which is undergoing that last moment of transformative agony before, upon slowly whirling to face the mugger, he becomes Charles Bronson.

This is the only scene that attempts to show the brutality of killing someone with a gun; in fact, thirty-six years later it retains its ugly power: the victim writhes, retches, grabs his wounded abdomen in terrible pain.

---

16. For those interested in seeing the way that overuse of close-ups can completely devalue their impact, a textbook example is Peter Jackson's *King Kong*.

Enter Ochoa

There is an overall shift in rhythm and narrative strategy that takes place when Ochoa enters at what's roughly the film's halfway point, which I'll talk about in greater detail toward the end of this chapter, though I want to mention it here. In order to accommodate the storyline of Ochoa's pursuit of Paul, *Death Wish* abruptly stops being a story for us, about a man's transformation, and starts being about efforts to hinder the transformed man, his evasion of those efforts, and about the way a denatured and incomplete version of "our" story enters the imaginations of other characters in the film—those of the police, primarily Ochoa, who intuitively understands what motivates the vigilante without knowing the details; that of the media, whose speculative coverage creates a new version of the story; and that of the public, whose fancy it captures.

Further, what had been a movie of serial episodes detailing Paul's heroic journey becomes a police procedural alternating with discrete but pornographically repetitive episodes portraying in detail his second job of baiting and killing criminals (he takes on the task as if he were moonlighting). Techniques unseen in the first half of the film—for example, the use of crosscutting—are employed frequently.

"By God and Jesus Christ, it's impossible."

Ochoa at the crime scene, and then in the precinct house rallying the troops. The film's use of space and the figures in it becomes particularly interesting when you compare Kersey's "public" scenes with Ochoa's. As I mentioned before, Kersey's scenes employ space to *centrifugal* effect; with Kersey and whomever he's talking to occupying the center of the frame, while all others move around him in a state of obliviousness, isolating him amid these crowds of people and lending the scenes a powerful feeling of estrangement, even alienation. Ochoa's scenes, by contrast, are *centripetal*—surrounding people focus on him, cluster near him; he is as constantly scrutinized as Kersey is overlooked.

"Crime is a police responsibility."

The commissioner's press conference with Ochoa. The centrifugal/centripetal effects are contrasted nicely here, with crosscutting between the actual press conference and the restaurant in which Paul sits anonymously, watching the event on TV with his coworkers as they eat.

More important, this is the first of several scenes in the film in which heavy media interest in the vigilante story is played up; part of what *Death Wish* is "about" is the porousness of the border separating lived experiences from mediated ones, and maybe also the border separating some mediated experiences from others. Myth is myth in *Death Wish*, even if certain differences between types of myth are exaggerated in order to conceal the equivalency. That is, Old Tucson's gunfights and New York's vigilante are processed through the same mythmaking apparatus[17]—a reasonable enough conjecture, and a fair enough evaluation of one by-product of popular journalism. *Death Wish* is a film that rather slickly adapts what Don DeLillo has called "the nausea of News and Traffic" in order to

17. "Print the legend."

provide a metafictional echo of its story, showing our way of experiencing events as stories and forming ideas through an ingrained process of mythopoesis that the movie itself embodies and, in several forms, depicts.

"How do you like your liver done?"

Jack arrives at Paul's apartment for dinner. The takeaway here is emotional; Winner splats us with everything he's got to convey the change that Paul has undergone. The apartment has been redone in garish orange paint, brassy music is blasting on the stereo, the camera pushes and pulls us, bullying us through the space, which is shot from completely different angles than in other scenes: a new apartment, as far as we're concerned.

The performances matter here; Keats is actually *more* hang-dog, *more* of a sad sack, than he has been; the scene opens on a close-up of the front door opening to admit him, and he stands bundled and hunched as if the hallway outside is freezing cold. Bronson, on the other hand, borrows his body language from Stuart Margolin's portrayal of Jainchill, so that the restraint in previous scenes at least *seems* to be exposed as a symptom of his prior inhibition. The two men have an abortive argument; Jack is angry because Paul doesn't seem appropriately upset by Carol's continuing decline. "What the hell do you want me to do?" Paul asks. "Moan and groan for the rest of my life?" But Paul has found a way, and a reason, to continue; "'Terror' is his epitaph," while Jack is stuck in the emotional bunker that is civilization.

Bronson's dinner offering—liver and spaghetti—is absurd enough to give the scene the comic dimension it needs, and his offer to make Jack a drink sounds faintly sultry (Jack immediately demurs): Could Paul possibly have seducing Jack on his mind? Well, it's fun to play with, anyway, particularly as actors play with various motivations to set an effective emotional pitch for a scene; why else (as long as we're here) would Paul get so angry when Jack immediately brings up Carol after turning down Paul's purred, "Hey, no drink? Let me make you one."

No matter. Bronson struts around comfortably; for the first time in the film he doesn't walk as if his feet hurt.

"Pussy Posse"

At the coffee shop. I wanted to mention this scene because of the ways it fails. There's the local-color problem, of course. As when Paul goes to the police station, here there's a surfeit of "types," with offbeat and "low" dialogue, etc. But like the Fifty-ninth Street Bridge, lit from behind by the sunset, the coffee shop is a big happy New York welcome, even with wisecracking whores making with pussy jokes. It may make nice people uncomfortable, but it isn't the Dark Portal, and it definitely isn't where Paul does his trolling.[18] Paul goes underground. Paul wanders into deserted parks. Paul strolls into dark alleys. Paul sits waiting in empty cars on the downtown local. And why is he "trolling" at all? Remember, *twenty-two seconds* for Dead

---

18. The setting is off, too. I wonder why Winner didn't take the opportunity to emphasize the link between *Death Wish* and the Western by placing the scene in a bar, one of those dives that used to dot Eighth Avenue. Really, the only thing missing would have been a player piano banging out "Oh! Susanna!"

Mugger #1 to make the fatal decision to stalk Paul. No, the movie fails in the name of variety here. Someone—Winner, maybe—worried, "Not enough New York stuff," and so we got a generically louche coffee shop out of the generic Seventies New York Photoplay playbook. Also, those point-of-view shifts I mentioned earlier: Why does the whore widen her eyes at the sight of Paul's roll? Winner wanted this, or he wouldn't have given her one of the handful of close-ups he doles out. Who cares? Does Paul see it? Is the whore going to mug him? Well, that's what "whores" do, I suppose is the movie's observation: they pick their noses and widen their eyes at the sight of money. I would guess that whores have a much more aloofly blasé attitude toward the sight of money (if not the stuff itself).

Finally, there's the problem of the two guys who do end up mugging him. If the nose-picking, eye-popping whore isn't going to mug him, who's left? Well, there are some nice people minding their own business, who don't seem to know that they're in the departure lounge for the Erinys Express, and there are some other whores just kicking back between blow jobs, I guess, and then there's that table with the black guys at it. Huh. Race doesn't loom nearly as large in the film as one might be led to believe, but really: something like this can leave a bad taste in your mouth.

"A few are fighting back"

Paul relaxes watching television and reading newspaper and magazine articles about himself after having shot the coffee shop muggers (one in the liver, nicely recalling his meal with Jack: How do you like your liver done? With a .32, thanks) in a subway underpass. That porousness, again: in the newscast Paul watches, television reporters talk with citizens who have fought back against street crime; in each of two incidents detailed, Winner cuts from the image of the reporter conducting a stand-up interview to show a filmed, soundless portrayal of the event being reported, the "citizen's" voice narrating the action, which is clearly intended to be construed as distinct from the newscast itself (the newscast footage is matted onto an image of the television screen in Paul's living room; the soundless footage occupies the entire frame). The fictive horizon of the film begins to recede: the nearest landmark on that horizon is Kersey in his living room; at a greater distance is the news program we watch him watching, recasting the event as a story; at the farthest remove is the story itself, represented by mysteriously omniscient footage of the citizen thwarting the crime, which *we* watch. But what engenders this third and most distant point on the horizon? Is it a flashback? Whose? Is it imagined? Is it imagined by Paul? By the entire television audience? Is it provided to us by Winner, to substitute for our own imaginations?

Two Contrasting Views of Order

VIEW #1:
  If they be two, they are two so
  As stiff twin compasses are two

At the police precinct, the number of suspects is narrowed to fourteen. Ochoa paces the squad room, lecturing; the cops gathered there lend him their complete attention. The camera obediently follows Ochoa as he strolls through the crowded room, reversing angle when he pauses in front of it and then following him back to his starting point. (Ochoa's Maigret routine bleeds a lot of the potency from the argument that *Death Wish* is an anti-police film[19]: Ochoa is competent, intuitive, articulate, and personable, his officers resourceful and dedicated to fulfilling his requests.) In the squad room, a central authority reigns, and an idea of order is enforced collectively through the will of one person.

VIEW #2:
> *The blood-dimmed tide is loosed, and everywhere*
> *The ceremony of innocence is drowned*

Even at Sam's party, a social occasion where his own secret actions are the main topic of conversation, Paul is alone. While Ochoa basically works a room, the camera tagging behind, the camera anticipates Paul's every move as he heads straight from entry to exit (Ives remarks, "He hasn't been the same since that terrible incident"—more cant hot off the newscast griddle: had the film been made today, it would be a "tragic" incident), leaving the room he has just entered to step out

---

19. That this argument sometimes was made in concert with the argument that it is a film espousing "fascism" illustrates the incoherent responses it was capable of eliciting. (Oddly, to my knowledge, no critic has complained about the fact that the search Ochoa makes of Paul's apartment, in which he finds evidence linking Paul to the shootings, is conducted illegally.)

onto the rooftop deck of Sam's apartment, standing alone to gaze out at the edge of Manhattan, hard by the icy Hudson. Where Ochoa's idea of order requires collaboration and coordination, Paul's requires only secrecy (as Christie Malry, novelist B.S. Johnson's retributive and ultimately terroristic malcontent, notes in his "codification" of his principles, "I act alone. I do not seek the assistance of anyone else whatsoever. I carry out only such actions as are within my own capabilities. I am a cell of one . . . My duty to myself is equally to attack and to survive to attack again"). There follow two completely discontinuous shots of the Manhattan skyline, each lasting precisely four seconds: the centrifuge, writ large. Ochoa, issuing his commands, is at the magnetic center of his world; he withdraws into his office to await their fulfillment. Kersey remains silent and gazes out at the farthest-flung reaches of a secret domain.

Death Wish Forever

The movie should have ended here, inconclusively, with these haunting, echoing shots of a quiescent city. It would have allowed for the possibility of a sequel without any of the ridiculous folderol necessary to bring Kersey out of "retirement" (*DW2*: Kersey's daughter is raped by thugs—again!—and leaps from a window to escape, impaling herself on a picket fence. *DW3*: Kersey returns to New York for a visit just in time to discover that an old friend has been murdered by thugs. *DW4*: Kersey's girlfriend's daughter dies of an overdose of crack sold to her by thugs. *DW5*: Kersey's fiancée is murdered by thugs trying to muscle in on her business). As it is, the rest of the film is essentially a simple cat-and-mouse game, with the added complication that Ochoa, having identified Paul as the prime suspect, is forbidden from arresting him by the police commissioner and the district attorney for fear of political repercussions.

Terribly, what the film loses is its peculiar treatment of temporality. In the first half, and in at least part of the second, *Death Wish* doesn't have much use for conventional time—while most of its sequences take place in a kind of cinematic "real time" (very few of them stitching together continuous yet abbreviated chains of events, as in the opening when the Kerseys fly home, ride through heavy traffic, arrive at their building, settle back into their routine, and then go to bed, compressing many hours of activity into a montage of about three minutes' length), it's a movie in which time as an essential element has been unseated. Its passage is unremarked-upon, or made deliberately vague: The duration of Paul's trip to Tucson is never even hinted at; while there, he's invited to the gun club by Jainchill, and is shown there in the scene immediately following, but after several viewings it becomes clear that it can't be the evening of Jainchill's initial invitation, since both men are dressed completely differently. The police make reference to the time-consuming nature of Inspector Ochoa's investigative strategy, but then presently recite the results of that investigation. Paul's apartment is shown first in its original state, then in the process of being redecorated, and then completed. Stories of vigilantism sprout on the covers of national newsweeklies and opinion magazines. Has a week gone by? A month? Two? It's a kind of mythic use of time and narrative in which, as Umberto Eco points out, it is impossible for the hero to be "consumed" because of the sustained "illusion of a continuous present."

Eco's points, made in "The Myth of Superman," are interesting. He notes that the difference between a traditional mythic figure like Hercules and a contemporary one is that the ancient story was already well established, and no matter what the embellishment added by the teller, the audience was told "the story of something which had already happened and of which the public was aware." Now, he says, the reader's main interest "is transferred to the unpredictable nature of *what will happen*." A contemporary hero—such as Paul Kersey—falls into a special trap that comes about because he must both be predictable, in the classical sense, but also endure the unforeseen, like a character in a novel, that pesky eighteenth-century literary and commercial development. Since both commercially and aesthetically the hero must go on, "There is nothing left to do except to put [him] to the test of several obstacles which are intriguing because they are unforeseen but which are, however, surmountable by the hero." Kersey becomes the star of his own comic book, with Ochoa as his opposite number, and after issue number one ("Origin of the Vigilante"), we settle into a routine.[20] Although the emergency presented in each episode is resolved, according to Eco, "this resolves nothing . . . Superman has still *accomplished*

---

20. "Alley Attack," "Subway Shooting," "Tunnel Trouble," "Panic in Riverside Park," and then "New Blood: Chicago," after which four actual sequels render imagination unnecessary.

something. Consequently, the character has made a gesture which is inscribed in his past and which weighs on his future. He has taken a step toward death . . . Superman is a myth on condition of being a creature immersed in everyday life . . . he possesses the characteristics of timeless myth, but is accepted only because his activities take place in our human and everyday world of time." While Superman's writers are able to solve the problem of the "irreversible premise" carrying their hero "another step toward his death" by creating an "oneiric climate . . . where what has happened before and what has happened after appear extremely hazy," *Death Wish* is a good illustration of the narrative crisis that can occur when genres are pushed together without a true synthesis occurring. The "oneiric climate," which is achieved quite nicely in the mythical-origin half of the film, is utterly disrupted by the equal weight given to the detective story starring Frank Ochoa. It's necessary for us to be made aware of the way time is weighing on the police as they search for the vigilante (scenes that seem to exist merely to impart information appear more frequently than in the first half, paradoxically, despite the fact that many of them could be eliminated from the film without much loss of coherence), but this awareness also signals to us that the film has a terminal point; such scenes serve as markers of narrative progression, pulling us toward the end credits. Yet Paul still seems to have slipped almost completely out of the flow of time. The contrast between these two competing "climates" gives a jumbled feeling to the second half of the film: you could, I suspect, rearrange many of its scenes willy-nilly without losing any narrative sense.

Riding its own dying momentum, *Death Wish* moves toward its conclusion; it becomes flaccid and without tension (see the crosscutting in the sequence where Paul sneaks away from his staked-out apartment to retrieve his gun from his office as Ochoa, realizing Paul has skirted the surveillance, tries to head him off there—as charismatic as Gardenia makes Ochoa, there's never any question that Paul will evade him). The remainder of the film has its moments: the encounter between Kersey and Ochoa at the hospital, with the movie's final winking reference to the old West (Ochoa: "We want you to get out of New York. Permanently." Kersey: "Inspector: By sundown?"); the iconic final scene, in which Paul, at Union Station in Chicago, for the first time deliberately enters the dreamy, somnambulistic background of one of those public shots to assist a woman being harassed by freaks (Chicago Chapter[21]), and grinningly points a gun formed from the fingers of his hand at them.

Those fingers not only pantomime a gun, but point toward the future: four sequels and innumerable urban revenge films, few of them improving on *Death Wish*'s model, many not complicated enough even to repeat its mistakes.

But there is something haunting about the original film: perhaps the too-grim-to-be-spoken assertion that Paul's loss is, in fact, a gain. Or perhaps it's the immense sense of loneliness it radiates, although for Kersey, friends are beside the

---

21. Outfitted even more absurdly than the three freaks, this crew has all the appurtenances of characters in a Gilbert Shelton comic.

point; the idea of family in this film seems to herald a remarkably common isolation—people sitting dwarfed by and alone in their huge rooms, entertaining nobody, seeing nobody; a Paul Kersey left so utterly alone that after his wife is murdered nobody even thinks to check up on his days and nights; and these are the conditions under which drugs or booze or even perhaps murder find you. And, as Kersey is found, he finds us. Like the Reverend Mr. Hooper, he is the blackened and obscured conscience walking amid, but outside, a community of self-styled piousness; a constant reminder of darkness.

EPILOGUE

Afterthoughts on the Middle Level

Among the epigraphs opening this book is one from Robert Warshow's essay "Movie Chronicle: The Westerner." I thought later that Warshow might well have written that popular culture itself presents, to the mind of his hypothetical "educated observer," ipso facto grounds for outright dismissal, and I took that as a warning to myself, especially since he also writes, in a passage coming a little before my epigraph, "[T]he 'vocabulary' of films is much larger than that of literature and falls more readily into pleasing or significant arrangements. (That may explain why the middle levels of excellence are more easily reached in the movies than in literary forms, and perhaps also why the status of the movies as art is constantly being called into question.)" I have been thinking about pop culture for decades now, in connection with my own work and in connection with my habits as a cultural consumer, and I find myself in the maybe antiquated position of believing, fervently, in the usefulness of maintaining a distinction between "high" and "low," while at the same time remaining suspicious of the kind of mummified thinking that will scrutinize examples of either only after having confined them to their respective enclosures. This is a somewhat oblique way of saying that I came to *Death Wish* with great interest, and a sense of familiarity, but without any long-held opinions and a vague preconception of the film as schlock—as in, "merely" schlock. It wasn't long before I realized that it was precisely this mindset that yielded the critical reactions I cite throughout this book. Well, that wouldn't do, and the project became, for me, a wonderful opportunity for ad hoc thinking. I found myself engaged in the best kind of struggle every day, and with only a handful of opinions to draw on—opinions that were often supercilious, affronted, lazy, or outright stupid—I actually had to LOOK at the movie, as Ezra Pound might have put it.

As some readers will have noticed, the book takes every opportunity to refute such critical reactions, if only because I can't accept as valid the observations of people who, having been paid to watch and write about a movie, regurgitated instead their most presentably upright sensibilities. What we have learned, from Vincent Canby and Andrew Sarris and Molly Haskell and Penelope Gilliatt and Roger Ebert and many lesser-known reviewers, is that *they are smarter than the people for whom they believe the movie was made.* Furthermore, *they are exemplary people*, because they know, for example, that *fascism is bad.* We also reap cinematic insight, such as the idea that *Charles Bronson should know his place*[22] and—an element essential to the critical *coup de maître*—*this movie just makes stuff*

---

22. Haskell: "Cro-Magnon Man"; Sarris: "the central credibility problem in *Death Wish:* the casting of Bronson as anything but a primitive form of life"; Canby: "Bronson . . . seems no more capable of intellectual activity than a very old, very tired circus bear."

up. Maybe most egregiously, we learn that *this movie is so dumb that none of these reviewers feels as if s/he really has to talk about it.*

So they didn't talk about it. To read about *Death Wish* is often to read about everything adjacent to the actual film. In maybe the most delicious case, *Village Voice* critic Sarris (in an incestuous bit of Downtown infighting in which he defends the *Voice* review written by Haskell, his wife, against the criticism of *Voice* photographer Fred W. McDarrah, expressed in a letter to the editor—of the *Voice*![23]) actually contributes a compulsive diatribe on his personal feelings about subway graffiti (thumbs down). I soon discovered that a good part of this project would entail pushing aside the attitudes engendered by the movie in order to get at the movie itself. Reviewers (both positive and negative) dismissed the film, and the occasional subsequent critic, while acknowledging its influence, has tended to stick it in a larger context, so that a given interpretation of the film exists to support the validity of that posited context[24]: very academic, which is something I am very much not, for better or worse. Not that I didn't find it useful to look at trends in filmmaking—"tendencies," as Robert B. Ray puts it—and not that I haven't clearly created my own context for *Death Wish*, or borrowed those of others when they've served my purpose. But the examination

---

23. In the memorable phrase of my beloved father, the whole thing reads "like the Brontë sisters arguing over a dildo."

24. My favorite is Nate Berg's post on the blog Planetizen drawing a connection between Paul Kersey and Jane Jacobs: "Both have important lessons to teach about what it means to be part of a neighborhood."

of overall tendencies necessarily plays down the sui generis aspects of individual films, and what is sui generis about *Death Wish* has been ignored or avoided by criticism of all kinds.

If *Death Wish* fails, it's because it's often slack and shoddy. That is to say, there is nothing *inherently* wrong with *Death Wish* as an idea, or as the exploration of a theme, or as a story. There's nothing forbidden or reprehensible or incorrect about it. No essentialist dogma informs our opinion of the work of Michael Winner, a journeyman if ever there was one. So *Death Wish* began to strike me as an illustrative instance of the tension that occurs when a filmmaker begins to become involved with the art of making, while at the same time remaining focused primarily on the goal of commercial success. The production of *Death Wish* was motivated by the prospect of making a lot of money; otherwise it wouldn't have been made.[25] So, Winner had no intention of making a work of art, yet at times *Death Wish* is unmistakably artful. There's no question of thwarted ambition here, or of Winner's contriving to sneak the good stuff in through the back door; there's simply enough talent in evidence to make you regretful when you've watched the film enough to be able to make a clear distinction between the lazy fizzle of workaday filmmaking and the carefully arrived at decisions of an artist.

---

25. *Death Wish* producer Dino De Laurentiis found this to be a motivating factor whomever the director. He told *The New York Times*, "Never set out to make a masterpiece . . . Fellini and I did *La Strada* for only two reasons—to entertain and to make money. Period."

Which brings me back to that old-fashioned commitment to high and low I mentioned, because paying and continuing to pay close attention to a work of art, any work of art, after first having forced yourself to transcend your initial, puerile, sense of superiority to the material, makes you hunker and think, mostly about the art in question, but also about the mandarin artificiality of viewing such divisions as absolute and impermeable. Most everyone has a distinctly uncritical susceptibility to thinking that some things have an Olympian glow to them, and that others don't. But while it's not quite as statistically quantifiable as the two percentage points that mark the difference between, say, a good hitter in baseball and a great one, a film like *Death Wish*, occupying the "middle levels" Warshow referred to, illustrates that works of art are sometimes, if not always, judged according to the ratio of success to failure that obtains in the sum of their individual parts. *Death Wish* fails a lot, but it didn't have to, and I eventually found its successes in unexpected places. This is what I guess is meant when something is said to "repay" repeated viewing, reading, listening. And *Death Wish* did repay my efforts. While I don't think that anything could have made it a great film—a determination that somehow makes me feel happier and more confident about the conclusions I've drawn here—it is significant unto itself, not as a progenitor of a genre, or as part of a larger trend or trends, or as a "symptom" of a breed of malaise that has long since entered that fairy tale book titled *The Seventies*, and I hope I've made clear my reasons for asserting that.

* * *

As I said at the outset, this book contradicts itself from time to time. Partly this is for the reason I mentioned—that scrutinizing the same things in different contexts can sometimes lead to divergent observations—but mostly I'm just not as interested in presenting an airtight thesis as I am in suggesting a whole bunch of ways of watching *Death Wish* (or maybe any film) that don't immediately bog it down in questions of right and wrong, questions of left and right, questions of reality versus fiction—perhaps especially questions of reality versus fiction.

A final note. Around the time that I was completing the chapter "*Death Wish* as Film," I came across a post written in 2007 by Tom Goulter for Ornery World, a blog. Here's what he had to say, in pertinent part:

> If you were explaining *Death Wish* or *The Brave One* to someone, what you'd say is that they're both about vigilantism. But if you were explaining at length, what you might actually say is that they're about how two characters, faced with similar circumstances, discover the narrative of street justice, and the process by which they give themselves over to becoming protagonists in a retelling of that narrative. What the movies are actually about is people faced with dire circumstances and electing to deal with the fallout by becoming characters in a prewritten story . . . What's weird about *Death Wish*—it being something of a genre-definer here—is how it just knows it has to have The Public Response as a major plot point . . . Both movies use the

device of media filtration of our character's actions to show that the narrative is now picking them up and sweeping them away, and both movies later use media-relayed citizen interviews to further that story, and add the element where The Common People make it their own.

But after similarly mythologized beginnings, snow-balling into similarly "traumatized citizen caught up in mythological whirlwind" narratives, what's lovely is how the two end: as polar opposites . . . What we might call the protagonists' material goal in both movies is clear: avenging their loved one's death. But the deeper goal both movies are concerned with is learning a way to keep on living.

Paul Kersey finds a way to keep on living, alright. He never makes any attempt to track down Jeff Goldblum's murderous Jughead lookalike: he just goes round killing folk until the Police run him out of town. The final frame, delightfully, has him smiling like a loon at the idea of having a whole new city full of ne'er-do-wells to callously gun down. His wife hasn't been avenged, his daughter's been indefinitely institutionalised . . . But none of that matters worth a whit to Paul—who, one feels, if you asked him, "so Paul, four more movies' worth of this sort of thing, eh?", would give that lazy laconic grin and ask where he could sign up.

I cite this not to cop to the unoriginality of my think-ing, or to congratulate myself and Mr. Goulter for agreeing in large part, or to suggest that the profundity of my observa-tions has been independently confirmed. I guess the reason I bring it up is because the way Goulter puts it, in a one-off post on a blog, without all the ceremony and self-celebration and ponderousness of researching and writing a 25,000-word monograph, it sounds like the most natural and self-evident set of offhand observations in the world. Which perhaps it is, which suggests that one key to thinking about a film is to watch it receptively, without preconceptions, absorbing it as a film, as a story, as a set of performances; as a concoction of things that bring other films, stories, performances, and ideas to mind. That the *professional*[26] reviewers who watched *Death Wish* in 1974 didn't manage to come up with any of these insights, or the variations on them that this book provides, unmistakably says that on some significant level they didn't watch the film, and I don't necessarily think it was their perception of the film's politics or attitudes that stopped them—although those things were conveniently used to club the movie, as was, mutatis mutandis, its popular success. We fail when we walk into a movie knowing in advance what we're going to see, and, having convinced ourselves, see only our preordained conclusions.

---

26. I make the distinction in deference to Andrew Sarris, who asserts that it is only professionals who are saddled with being "ultimately account-able for what little remains of conscience in the exploitation of screen spectacles." This in a piece titled "Death Wish: The Final Solution?"

APPENDIX

Synopsis

Paul Kersey (Charles Bronson) and his wife, Joanna (Hope Lange), relax on a beach in Hawaii, where they are vacationing. "I don't want to go home," Joanna tells Paul. We soon see why: they return to New York in the dead of winter, a city beset by traffic jams, gray skies, crowds, and, as Paul's coworker Sam (William Redfield) immediately reminds him when he returns to his job as a development engineer, rampant crime.

Later that same day, Joanna goes grocery shopping with her and Paul's adult daughter, Carol (Kathleen Tolan). Three young men (Jeff Goldblum, Christopher Logan, Gregory Rozakis) spot them and, reading Joanna's address off a delivery slip, stalk them to the Kersey apartment building, where they gain entry through a service door and pose as deliverymen from the supermarket. When Carol admits them, the three rob the two women, vandalize the apartment, and then beat Joanna severely and sexually assault Carol. Paul is informed of the assault in a telephone call from his son-in-law, Jack Toby (Steven Keats), who tells Paul to meet him at the hospital. There, after receiving a frustratingly sketchy report on the attack from the police officer on the scene (Robert Kya-Hill), Paul is informed that Joanna has died.

Carol begins to recede into a catatonic state arising from the trauma of the assault, and when, after Joanna's funeral, Paul goes to the local police precinct to talk with the detective in charge of the case (Ed Grover), he is told that there is only a slim chance of apprehending the perpetrators. Paul soon is moved to obtain two rolls of quarters, which he places in a sock. When he is confronted by a mugger one evening on the way home, he strikes the mugger with the homemade weapon, sending him running.

Shortly thereafter, Paul is sent by his boss (Chris Gampel) to Tucson, Arizona, to supervise a development project that appears to be at risk of losing the firm's investment. There he meets the developer, Ames Jainchill (Stuart Margolin), and is gradually won over to the garrulous and persuasive Jainchill's views on everything from land development to the Western lifestyle to gun ownership. Jainchill takes Paul to Old Tucson, a tourist attraction, where with growing interest Paul watches a mock gunfight in which a marshal triumphs over three bank robbers. Over the next few weeks, Paul works to achieve a compromise between Jainchill's vision of "space for living" that "conforms to the land" and his firm's need for profitability, all the while assimilating the values and ethics of the Southwestern community, a process that culminates in Paul's acceptance of Jainchill's invitation to dine with him at the gun club to which he belongs. On the club's range, when Jainchill asks him about his wartime service, Paul advises him that he served as a conscientious objector in Korea. Jainchill laughs and mildly rebukes Paul, telling him "this is gun country," but then is surprised and impressed when Paul hits a bull's-eye with his first shot. Paul then informs him that he is very familiar with guns, had grown up with "all kinds of guns," but that his mother's pacifist leanings had checked his enthusiasm. After his father was killed in a hunting accident, Paul fully embraced his mother's beliefs.

Having successfully completed his duties in Arizona, Paul returns to New York. A grateful Jainchill stows a gift in Paul's luggage. When Paul arrives at Kennedy Airport, he's met by Jack, who tells him that Carol's condition has grown worse and that she needs to be committed to an institution. After visiting her, Paul returns to his apartment, where he finds that photographs from the Hawaii trip have arrived in the mail. After gazing at the pictures with evident emotion, he begins to unpack, coming upon Jainchill's gift. Removing the wrapping, he discovers that Jainchill has given him a .32-caliber revolver, which he examines thoughtfully.

Later that evening, Paul leaves his apartment building and walks purposefully to nearby Riverside Park. He is soon accosted by a mugger, who threatens his life at gunpoint. Paul shoots the man to death and then runs home, where he vomits with revulsion at what he's done. The next morning, Inspector Frank Ochoa (Vincent Gardenia) arrives at the scene of the murder in Riverside Park, discussing the crime with other policemen and theorizing about the circumstances. Paul continues his activities, killing three men who are beating up a fourth in an alley. Ochoa soon links this incident with the earlier one.

Paul and Jack bring Carol to the mental hospital outside

the city where she will be committed. As they wait for a train to take them back to New York, Jack laments that they should have abandoned the violence of the city for such an area long ago. Paul demurs, suggesting that the answer is to fight back.

Meanwhile, Ochoa plans strategy with his officers, suggesting that they narrow the investigation to focus on members of the public who have had family members killed by muggers. He acknowledges the seeming impossibility of the task but suggests that the work will keep the police busy and placate the media, which already has seized upon the case and made "the Vigilante," so-called, a cause célèbre. Undeterred, or encouraged, by his growing notoriety, Paul continues, killing two men who attack him on a subway train and then disappearing into the crowds on the street. The police commissioner (Stephen Elliott) soon holds a news conference that is attended by both local and international reporters. Paul watches the event on television as he eats lunch with his colleagues in a restaurant, smiling as the commissioner urges the vigilante to turn himself in.

Paul has left a bag of groceries behind after the shooting on the subway, and the police identify the store where the groceries were purchased, narrowing the radius of their investigation to Paul's immediate neighborhood. Paul, meanwhile, grows ever more buoyant and confident, redecorating his apartment in bold colors and playing jaunty brass music loudly on his stereo.

Paul next shoots and kills two muggers in an underground passage in a subway station after having baited them by flashing a wad of cash at a coffee shop. One of the muggers manages to stab him before Paul shoots him. Returning home, Paul dresses his wound and then leafs through newspaper and magazine coverage of his exploits while watching television news, which reports that ordinary citizens are beginning to fight back against street crime. He later attends a cocktail party, where the mysterious vigilante's actions are also the primary topic of discussion.

Having come up with Paul's name on his list of possible suspects, Ochoa illegally searches his apartment for clues, coming across the bloodied cotton Paul used to clean his knife wound, which he compares with blood taken from the knife. Certain that he has his man, he orders Paul placed under round-the-clock surveillance, but first is told by the police commissioner and the district attorney (Fred J. Scollay) that if he has identified Paul as a prime suspect, he is not to apprehend him: muggings have dropped by more than half, and the officials fear an epidemic of vigilantism if news gets out, and don't want a martyred Paul in custody. Ochoa agrees reluctantly to try to scare him off, first phoning Paul anonymously to let him know that he is under surveillance and then arranging to have three police officers roust and frisk him as he walks home. Later that evening, Paul evades Ochoa and his partner by leaving through the service entrance of his apartment building and heads to his office, where he's stored his gun. Ochoa realizes that he's been given the slip but narrowly misses Paul when he attempts to intercept him at the office.

Paul returns to Riverside Park, where he is confronted by three muggers who box him in by standing at opposite ends of the staircase he is descending. He successfully shoots two of them, but is shot by the third, whom he then pursues to a waterfront complex, but collapses from his wound just as the police arrive. Ochoa arrives at the scene and speaks to a young officer, Patrolman Reilly (Christopher Guest), who shows him the gun that he has confiscated from Paul. After extracting a promise from Reilly not to mention the gun on his official report, Ochoa goes to see Paul at the hospital, where he tells him that he will drop the gun in the river if Paul agrees to put in for a transfer to one of his firm's other offices and leave New York permanently.

Paul arrives by train in Chicago, where he is greeted at the station by a member of the firm. While the two talk, Paul notices a young woman being harassed by a group of young men. He goes over to assist her, and the men yell at him and gesture obscenely. The final image of the film is of Paul grinning at the men as he forms a pistol with the fingers of his right hand and aims it at them.

ACKNOWLEDGMENTS

Thanks are due to Alex Abramovich, Ira Silverberg, Denise Oswald at Soft Skull, and to the Deep Focus series editor, Sean Howe, for suggesting the project and for providing, along with his co-dedicatees Andrew Hultkrans and Jonathan Lethem, continuous kibitzing on this and many other subjects.

I would also like to thank the New York State Department of Labor, Unemployment Insurance Division, and the Victoria Sorrentino Fund for Indigent Middle-aged Writers, for partially subsidizing the writing of this book.

The thought on page 55 that runs, in part, "perhaps because it had so thoroughly desublimated his onscreen presence he was never as useful or effective again," is lifted nearly verbatim from an e-mail to the author from Jonathan Lethem.

Printed in the United States
by Baker & Taylor Publisher Services